CRIMINAL JUSTICE

Crime and Criminals

CRIMINAL JUSTICE

Crime and Criminals

Crime Fighting and Crime Prevention

Evidence

The Law

Prison and the Penal System

Trials and the Courts

CRIMINAL JUSTICE

Crime and
Criminals

Michael Newton

CHELSEA HOUSE
PUBLISHERS
An imprint of Infobase Publishing

CRIMINAL JUSTICE: Crime Fighting and Crime Prevention

Chelsea House
An imprint of Infobase Publishing
132 West 31st Street
New York NY 10001

Library of Congress Cataloging-in-Publication Data

Newton, Michael, 1951-
Crime and criminals / Michael Newton.
p. cm. — (Criminal justice)
Includes bibliographical references and index.
ISBN-13: 978-1-60413-628-9 (hardcover : alk. paper)
ISBN-10: 1-60413-628-6 (hardcover : alk. paper) 1. Crime. 2. Criminals.
I. Title. II. Series.
HV6025.N495 2010
364—dc22   2009035686

Chelsea House books are available at special discounts when purchased in bulk quantities for businesses, associations, institutions, or sales promotions. Please call our Special Sales Department in New York at (212) 967-8800 or (800) 322-8755.

You can find Chelsea House on the World Wide Web at http://www.chelseahouse.com

Text design by Erika Arroyo
Cover design by Keith Trego
Composition by Kerry Casey
Cover printed by Bang Printing, Brainerd, MN
Book printed and bound by Bang Printing, Brainerd, MN
Date printed: March 2010

Printed in the United States of America

10 9 8 7 6 5 4 3 2 1

This book is printed on acid-free paper.

All links and Web addresses were checked and verified to be correct at the time of publication. Because of the dynamic nature of the Web, some addresses and links may have changed since publication and may no longer be valid.

Contents

Introduction

No one on Earth today escapes the touch of crime. Without regard to race, religion, sex, or nationality, each human being on the planet is affected negatively by the acts of criminals. Everyone feels the impact of crime every day whether they know it or not.

Small businesses see profits lost to shoplifters, while huge corporations suffer embezzlement by trusted employees—or face criminal prosecution when companies themselves break the law. Reckless drivers and fraudulent insurance claims increase the rates everyone pays for insurance on cars and other property. Legitimate firms pay "protection" or "taxes" to organized crime and then recover their losses by raising consumer prices. Drug addicts rob strangers and burglarize homes to support their habits, while wealthy narcotics dealers bribe police and politicians. Those corrupted, in turn, abuse their authority and the citizens whom they are sworn to serve.

In some extreme cases, a crime may even change the course of history.

On January 14, 1914, an assassin murdered Archduke Franz Ferdinand and his wife in Sarajevo, now the capital of Bosnia and Herzegovina. The killing was supposed to protest Serbia's domination by Austria-Hungary, but it ignited existing tensions and sparked the First World War instead, claiming more than 18.6 million lives by 1918, while more than 34 million were wounded.[1] Whole empires collapsed, revolution changed Russia forever, and treaties signed to end the fighting paved the way for even greater bloodshed during World War II—all events set in motion partly by a single murder

Some historians speculate that another assassination—that of United States President John F. Kennedy in November 1963—had a similar effect on history. Kennedy had spoken of withdrawing American military forces from the Asian country of South Vietnam, but his successor, Vice President Lyndon Johnson, chose to escalate that conflict during 1964-68, as did President Richard Nixon in 1969-71. By the time the last U.S. soldiers finally left Vietnam, 58,217 had been killed, another 1,947 were missing, and 153,457 had been wounded. Estimates of the native Vietnamese death toll range from 500,000 to more than 2 million.[2]

While no rational person welcomes crime, some historians argue that specific criminal acts have also *helped* society. One case often cited is the Ku Klux Klan bombing of Birmingham, Alabama's Sixteenth Street Baptist Church in September 1963, which killed four young girls in their Sunday school class. Fourteen years passed before the first bomber was brought to justice in court, but meanwhile, the horror aroused by his crime broke a longstanding deadlock in Congress, resulting in passage of the 1964 Civil Rights Act that guaranteed equal treatment for African Americans after decades of racial discrimination. Without the bombing and other acts of racist violence, some contend, that law might have been further postponed, or even defeated.[3]

In most American elections since the 1960s, candidates have raised crime as a major issue, promising to end it—or, at least, *reduce* it—if elected. Some of those who made that promise later were revealed as criminals themselves, and none has yet achieved the goal of making average Americans feel completely safe from crime at home or on the streets.

Crime has a human face. According to the Federal Bureau of Investigation (FBI), 131,227 persons were murdered in America between 2000 and 2007. During the same period 1,377 police officers died in the line of duty, at least 652,869 victims were raped, and 6,997,476 more suffered serious assaults. No reliable crime statistics exist for the world at large, but terrorist attacks alone claimed at least 65,130 lives around the world during the same eight years.[4] Each victim lost was someone's parent, child, sibling, spouse, lover, or friend.

Investigating crimes, identifying those responsible, and meting out their punishment costs American taxpayers billions of dollars each year.

The human cost in suffering defies calculation.

Before a problem can be solved, it must be understood. Nothing is gained from fearing or denouncing crime, unless its causes and the ways in which lawbreakers operate are understood. Without that basic knowledge—education in advance of action—and a solid plan for change, an angry speech denouncing crime is simply wasted breath.

Since no one can avoid crime's impact in the modern world, it is important to learn the history of criminal behavior and the motives of the individuals who prey upon society. Forearmed with knowledge, people may then attempt to change conditions that lead some to choose a criminal career, while dealing more effectively with those already launched upon a life of crime.

Crime and Criminals surveys the scope of modern crime and dangers posed by criminal activity in the United States and in the world at large. Chapters examine both the history of crime and major types of crime that plague society.

Chapter 1, "A World of Crime," examines trends in crime throughout America and foreign lands.

Chapter 2, "Original Sins," charts the history of criminal activity from ancient times to the present, tracking the evolution of lawless behavior.

Chapter 3, "Crimes of Violence," reviews the threat of violent criminals from shattered families and chance encounters to the systematic mayhem practiced by organized crime and global terrorists.

Chapter 4, "Drugs and Crime," examines the impact of illegal drugs on individuals and society at large, together with the ongoing debate over legalization of controlled substances.

Chapter 5, "Commercial Crimes," surveys crimes committed for profit, from petty theft to white-collar conspiracies and the threat of "kleptocracy," or whole governments run by thieves for their personal benefit.

Chapter 6, "Corrupting Authority," describes how criminals survive and prosper by bribing government officials and law enforcement officers sworn to oppose them.

Chapter 7, "Crimes Against Humanity," details the actions of criminals driven by hatred of large groups, including whole races and religions, sometimes resulting in mass-murder.

Chapter 8, "Cybercrimes," follows the advance of criminal activity into the age of computers and virtual reality.

Chapter 9, "Punishing Crime," explores the many different methods used to reduce or eliminate crime throughout history.

A World of Crime

Los Angeles, California

Edwin Rivera displayed the first symptoms of mental illness in 1999, after his mother died. Nine years later, on February 6, 2008, he shot and killed his father and two brothers at their home in the San Fernando Valley, then telephoned police to report the murders. Members of the Los Angeles Police Department's SWAT team quickly surrounded Rivera's house, evacuating neighbors, and a standoff ensued, broken at midnight when commanding officers gave an order to storm the residence.

Officer Randall Simmons was first through the door, followed closely by Officer James Veenstra. Rivera shot them both, killing Simmons and severely wounding Veenstra. Other members of the SWAT team then retreated, and the siege continued until 5:00 A.M. on February 7, when tear gas shells set the house afire. A female hostage emerged moments later, followed by Edwin Rivera—still shooting until a police sniper killed him.

Court records revealed that Rivera was convicted of assault with a firearm in 2004 but received probation because the gun was unloaded. Officers visited the Rivera home repeatedly in 2005 and 2006, responding to domestic arguments, but no further arrests were made. The four murders committed by Rivera brought L.A.'s death toll to 91 in the first five weeks of 2008.[1]

Los Angeles Police Chief William Bratton speaks at a February 2008 news conference about Edwin Rivera, the gunman who fatally shot a SWAT officer and three members of his own family. *AP Photo/ Nick Ut*

Anchorage, Alaska

Theodore Stevens was 45 years old in December 1968, when Alaska Governor Walter Hickel appointed him to fill a vacancy in the U.S. Senate, created by the death of Edward Bartlett. Alaska voters returned Stevens to Washington in 1970, 1972, 1978, 1984, 1990, 1996, and 2002. He was the Senate's longest-serving Republican by July 2008, when a federal grand jury indicted him on seven counts of failure to report gifts valued at $250,000. In return for those gifts, FBI agents claimed that Stevens had steered millions of taxpayers' dollars to companies owned by his personal friends.

Stevens proclaimed his innocence, but jurors convicted him on all seven felony counts in October 2008. Despite that conviction and Governor Sarah Palin's call for his immediate resignation, Stevens still sought re-election to an eighth Senate term on November 4, 2008. Stevens lost that election to Democratic opponent Mark Begich, but 137,937 Alaska voters ignored his conviction and likely future imprisonment, casting their ballots for his re-election.[2]

People's Republic of China

On July 16, 2008, Chinese authorities announced that 16 infants in Ganlu Province had developed kidney stones after consuming powdered milk produced by the Sanlu Group, a dairy products company based in Shijiazhuang. Investigators found that Sanlu had "improved" its powdered milk by adding the chemicals maltodextrin (derived from wheat, often used as a food additive) and melamine (normally found in pesticides and fire-retardant substances), which may cause bladder cancer in addition to the kidney stones experienced by the infant, Chinese victims.

The scandal swiftly spread, with four children reported dead and 94,000 hospitalized by September 2008.[3] Sanlu was not alone in spiking food products with melamine. In fact, 21 other manufacturers had done the same thing, on a smaller scale. Sanlu made matters worse, however, by asking Chinese authorities to censor media reports of the scandal. Despite accusations of past cover-ups, including government suppression of news concerning severe acute respiratory syndrome in 2002 and tainted pet foods in 2007, officials refused to cooperate. Sanlu general manager Tian Wenhua was held on criminal charges, along with 35 other traders and dairy farmers involved in the melamine case. Beyond those arrests, eight public officials lost their jobs, including China's Director of the Administration of Quality Supervision, Inspection and Quarantine.

Aside from powdered milk, the taint of melamine was also found in cheese, candy, cookies, and pastries shipped to Australia, Japan, Taiwan, Italy, Singapore, Thailand, Switzerland, and Vietnam. By October 2008 the European Union and 15 other individual countries, including the United States and Canada, plus nations in South America, Africa, and Asia, had banned or restricted importation of dairy-related products from China. While proceeding with the trial of 36 criminal suspects, Chinese officials denounced the bans as a case of "Western hysteria."

A health inspector explains the harms of Sanlu milk powder tainted with melamine to local villagers. By November 2008, China reported an estimated 300,000 victims affected by the tainted milk, formula, and other food materials and components, including six infant deaths from kidney stones or other kidney damage. *Imagechina via AP Images*

On December 1, 2008, Beijing acknowledged that tainted milk had killed six children and injured 300,000.[4]

The cases cited here are but a sampling of the crimes recorded in 2008. They illustrate how relatively simple acts—a quarrel with relatives, an effort to repay political favors, or a bid to boost corporate profits—may backfire with unexpected, even tragic consequences. It is evident that no one on the planet can avoid contact with crime, even if that crime is an act conceived by criminals halfway around the world.

But how else do such crimes affect people every day?

CRIME AT HOME

Most people think of home as a place to relax and escape the cares of the outside world, but crime threatens every family from coast to coast.

In 2007—the last year with full statistics available at this writing—the FBI reported 1,479,636 residential burglaries in the United States, resulting in property losses of $2.9 billion, or an average of $1,959 per break-in. During the same year, arson fires damaged or destroyed 24,549 homes, for an average loss of $17,289 per incident. Across the country, 1,095,769 motor vehicles were stolen, for an estimated loss of $7.4 million.[5]

Monetary losses pale beside the loss of human life. During 2007, American arson fires resulted in 295 deaths, including those of two firefighters killed while battling blazes that were deliberately set.[6] Most of those deaths were unintended by the fire-setters, but they are legally classified as murders.

The U.S. Department of Justice recorded 594,276 deliberate homicides nationwide between 1976 and 2005. Of those victims, 441,019 were killed in or near their homes, while another 67,580 were slain at the home of a friend or neighbor. A total of 64,529 victims were killed by intimate partners, defined as present or former spouses, boyfriends, or girlfriends. In that group, females were the most frequent victims: 33 percent of girls and women slain, versus 3 percent of males. During 2005 alone, 810 victims were slain by intimate partners, 271 by parents, 136 by siblings, 479 by their own children, 356 by other relatives, and 4,783 by a friend or acquaintance.[7]

Americans are most disturbed, it seems, when children fall prey to domestic violence. In 2006 the National Child Abuse and Neglect Data System recorded 1,530 deaths resulting from various forms of abuse nationwide. Children below the age of four accounted for 78 percent of those deaths (with 44.2 percent below the age of one), while 22 percent of the victims ranged from age four to their teens. Direct physical abuse, such as beating, shaking, or drowning, produced 343 deaths, while 629 resulted from neglect alone, and 558 were caused by combined abuse and neglect. Of the identified offenders, 76 percent were parents of the victims, 15 percent were non-parental caretakers, and relationships were unclear in 9 percent of the cases. Homicide statistics for 1976-2005 reveal that 31 percent of all murdered children were killed by their fathers, 29 percent by their mothers, 7 percent by other relatives, 23 percent by male acquaintances, and 3 percent by strangers.[8]

CRIME AT SCHOOL

Teenage killers Eric Harris and Dylan Klebold made global headlines on April 20, 1999, when they shot 46 victims at Colorado's Columbine High School, killing 13, before they committed suicide. The massacre climaxed a grim series of shootings in American schools, which resulted in 22 other slayings between 1996 and 1998.[9]

While homicides at schools are relatively rare, the Department of Justice reports that 15,450 victims were murdered on school grounds between 1976 and 2005.[10] Most died in individual attacks, rather than dramatic mass-shootings, but the numbers demonstrate that institutions of learning are not immune to violent crime.

"CRIME WARS"

American politicians often declare "war" on problems that trouble society, including poverty, cancer, and crime. President Franklin Roosevelt and Attorney General Homer Cummings ordered the first "war on crime" in June 1933, after four lawmen died in a shootout with gangsters in Kansas City, Missouri. Congress responded with new laws that broadened the FBI's powers and added federal penalties for various crimes, including bank robbery, interstate transportation of stolen property, and flight across state lines to avoid prosecution. Those laws, according to the FBI's Web site, "resulted in the arrest or demise of all the major gangsters by 1936."[11] In fact, however, while those killed or captured were dangerous felons with loosely knit gangs, none were members of organized crime as we know it today.

President Richard Nixon declared "war on drugs" in June 1971, launching a campaign pursued by the next six U.S. presidents at great expense, but with mixed results. Ignoring the cost to state and local law enforcement, the U.S. federal government spends $600 *per second* to investigate and prosecute drug-related crimes, arresting a drug-law violator every 17 seconds, on average. As of June 2008, the last year with full

An estimated 54.8 million students were enrolled at American schools, between prekindergarten and grade 12, for the 2005-06 school year. During that year, school officials recorded 14 homicides and three suicides. Another 1.5 million students between the ages of 12 and 18 were victims of nonfatal crimes, including 628,000 violent attacks and 868,100 reported thefts. Across America, 86 percent of all public schools recorded at least one crime on campus. Eight percent of high school students reported being injured or threatened with a weapon, 36 percent engaged in fights, 25 percent saw illegal drugs on campus, 5 percent smoked marijuana at school, and 4 percent admitted drinking alcoholic beverages on school grounds. Campus bullies terrorized 28 percent of all students age 12 to 18.[17]

statistics available, 20 percent of all inmates in America's state prisons—253,300 inmates—were confined for drug offenses.[12]

But does it help? Despite tremendous effort and expenditures, barely 13 percent of the world's illegal opium crop was seized by authorities in 2006.[13] During the same year, an estimated 2.4 million Americans used powdered cocaine, while some 702,000 smoked crack cocaine.[14] The price of heroin declined from $1,974.49 per gram in 1981 to $361.95 per gram in 2003, while average purity increased from 11 percent to 32 percent—proof positive of increased illegal supplies.[15]

In May 2009 President Barack Obama named Gil Kerlikowske Director of the White House Office on National Drug Control Policy, the nation's sixth "drug czar," to break that cycle. Kerlikowske told reporters in May 2009 that he hoped to banish the notion of a "war on drugs" and shift government attention toward treatment for drug addicts. He said, "Regardless of how you try to explain to people it's a 'war on drugs' or a 'war on a product,' people see a war as a war on them. We're not at war with people in this country."[16] It remains to be seen if changing attitudes in Washington can affect street-level reality.

RATING CRIME

Governments collect crime statistics in order to gauge the levels of crime in society, to chart trends over time, and to measure the effectiveness of various crime-fighting programs. Most statistics are reported by law enforcement agencies, but other sources include household surveys, insurance records, and hospital records. Various organizations, including the FBI, Britain's Home Office, Interpol, and the United Nations, publish crime statistics at regular intervals.

Although methods sometimes vary, most reporting agencies collect statistics in three broad areas: types of crimes reported, criminal offenders (classified by race, sex, age, and other factors), and victims (ranked in the same categories as criminals). Problems in comparison arise between different jurisdictions and legal systems, where certain acts may or may not be illegal. Thus, a state or country where gambling and prostitution are permitted may report no arrests in those categories, while others file numerous charges. Critics of statistical reporting also note that many crimes are not reported to police, including an estimated 60 percent of rapes committed across America in any given year.[18]

Recording practices for crime statistics vary greatly in different areas, sometimes influenced by politicians or police who are concerned about their reputations. Hate crimes are a case in point in the United States. The federal Hate Crime Statistics Act of 1990 orders FBI headquarters to collect reports

Pursuit of higher education is somewhat safer in America, but students and faculty still face threats from campus criminals. In 2007 the FBI collected crime statistics from colleges and universities in 44 states (minus Hawaii, Idaho, Illinois, Montana, New Hampshire, and Oregon), revealing 2,691 violent crimes reported on campus. Those offenses included 12 homicides and 471 forcible rapes.[19]

of hate crimes nationwide, but does not require state or local police to submit statistics. Some states file no reports with the FBI, while others omit notorious cases reported by the media nationwide.[20]

Crime statistics may also be manipulated by politicians or police officials for personal ends. Incumbent office holders sometimes use declining crime rates to support their re-election bids, while rising crime statistics make them vulnerable to opponents running on a "law-and-order" platform. Law enforcement agencies sometimes use crime statistics to support their pleas for increased funding, new equipment, and new officers. Former FBI Director J. Edgar Hoover was a master of statistical manipulation, often claiming credit for recovery of stolen cars retrieved by state and local police, sometimes even fabricating "crime waves" to support his pleas for larger budgets.[21]

Even with honest reporting, crime statistics are open to varied interpretation. Does a rise in arrests for drug possession suggest increasing drug sales or simply a shift in police priorities? What impact do cultural factors have on crime rates between separate nations dominated by different religions or political systems? If two-thirds of all rapes are unreported, does a statistical rise or drop in rape arrests mean anything at all? Scholars, politicians, and law enforcement officers have debated these and similar questions for decades. Definitive answers remain elusive.

CRIME AT WORK

On August 20, 1986, Patrick Sherrill carried two .45-caliber pistols to his job at the U.S. Post Office in Edmond, Oklahoma, killing 14 coworkers and wounding six more before he turned a gun on himself. That incident was one of 15 shootings by postal employees in eight states, between 1983 and 2006, which claimed 43 lives and left 23 victims wounded. As a result of those killings, the phrase "going postal" became common slang for public mayhem.[22]

Despite that series of flamboyant crimes, the Postal Service holds no monopoly on workplace violence. According to the Justice Department, 23,550 victims were killed in commercial business establishments across America, between 1976 and 2005. A separate study revealed that 2,009,400 persons were attacked or threatened in the workplace during 1992-96. The crimes for those five years included 1,000 homicides, 51,000 rapes, 84,000 robberies, 396,000 aggravated assaults, and 1.45 million simple assaults. Those suffering the most nonfatal incidents included law enforcement officers (431,200), retail employees (331,600), medical personnel (160,800), teachers (148,800), mental health workers (102,500), and transportation workers (76,500).[23]

While those statistics may be shocking, the vast majority of workplace crime is economic, involving theft of money or merchandise. The "petty" crime of shoplifting cost American retail stores $40.5 billion in 2007. Researcher Sherri Granato claims that 75 percent of all U.S. adults have practiced the "five-finger discount" at some time in their lives.[24] Consumers suffer when retailers pay higher insurance premiums and pass the cost on to their customers through increased prices.

Meanwhile, businesses also suffer from crimes committed by their own employees. In an average year, according to the American Management Association, companies lose $10 billion from employee pilferage, another $10 billion from commercial bribery (illegal kickbacks), $5 billion from stock theft or fraud, $4 billion from embezzlement of cash, $2.5 billion from vandalism, $2 billion from insurance and workers' compensation fraud, and $1.3 billion from fires set by angry workers. That report suggests that 15 to 30 percent of the price on some retail items represents recovery of such losses. The AMA also says that one-fifth of the firms that go bankrupt each year are driven out of business by their own criminal employees.[25]

THIEVES' WORLD

Such problems, of course, are not confined to the United States. The international nature of modern banking and finance, commerce and corporate activity, ensures that crime's impact is felt around the world, from the largest cities to the smallest rural villages. Computer technology permits thieves to rob banks in foreign countries without ever leaving their homes. Drug-dumping by Western pharmaceutical companies and corruption among Third World leaders brings misery and death to millions in Asia, Africa, and South America. Illegal traffic in nuclear weapons from former communist nations offers terrorists the potential opportunity to kill millions in a single attack. Environmental crimes threaten endangered species, the quality of air and water, and perhaps even the survival of the earth itself.

Two cases—those of Robert Calvi and Victor Bout—illustrate the disastrous impact that individual felons may have on the planet at large.

Calvi was a native of Milan, born in 1920, who served as chairman of Italy's second-largest private bank, Banco Ambrosiano, from 1975 to 1982. His close contacts with Rome's Vatican Bank earned him the nickname "God's Banker," but his conduct was far from saintly. In 1981 he was convicted of violating Italian law by smuggling $27 million out of the country and investing funds in foreign companies, including some with ties to organized crime. Despite a four-year suspended jail sentence and a $19.8 million fine, Banco Ambrosiano retained Calvi as chairman. On June 18, 1982, a British postman found Calvi hanging from Blackfriar's Bridge in London, the pockets of his clothing stuffed with bricks and $15,000 in cash. Banco Ambrosiano declared bankruptcy the following week, reporting losses of $1.3 billion. In 1984 the Vatican Bank compensated Banco Ambrosiano depositors with $224 million, admitting "moral involvement" in the bank's collapse.[26]

Authorities first listed Calvi's death as suicide then changed their verdict to murder after two coroner's inquests and a private investigation. Italian police charged five suspects with Calvi's slaying, but jurors in Rome acquitted all five at their trial in June 2007. Meanwhile, some researchers claimed that Calvi's crimes may have led to the alleged murder of Pope John Paul I in 1978 (officially listed as death from heart failure).

Victor Bout, a native of Tajikistan born in 1967, served as a major in the Russian army until 1993, when he retired to become an international arms dealer. The collapse of communism in 1991 left millions of weapons adrift in former Soviet states, and Bout took full advantage of that situation. Using his army contacts and fluency in six languages he became a mega-millionaire. Operating cargo airlines from Belgium, Florida, and the United Arab Emirates, he shipped weapons to war-torn nations, including Afghanistan, Angola, Cameroon, the Central African Republic, Colombia, the Democratic Republic of the Congo, Equatorial Guinea, Kenya, Liberia, Libya, the Republic of the Congo, Rwanda, Sierra Leone, Somalia, Sudan, Swaziland, and Uganda.

Prizing profit over ideology, Bout often sold arms to both sides in the same civil war, earning a global reputation as the "Merchant of Death." Despite protests, the United States government used Bout to arm some of its friends abroad until 2001, when informants claimed that he sold arms to al-Qaeda terrorists. Facing criminal charges from

Illegal arms dealer Victor Bout sits in a jail cell as he is processed in Bangkok, Thailand in March 2008 after being apprehended in a sting operation. On August 11, 2009, a Thai judge ruled in favor of Bout, denying the United States its request for extradition based on lack of legal basis and political motivation for the case. *AP Photo/ David Longstreath*

Interpol, Belgium, and U.S. authorities, Bout fled to Russia, whose constitution forbids extradition of Russian citizens to any foreign country.

In early 2008, Colombian authorities captured a computer owned by leftist guerrillas which linked them to Bout. Cooperating with agents of the U.S. Drug Enforcement Administration (DEA), they lured Bout to Thailand, supposedly to close a deal for sale of 200,000 AK-47 assault rifles. Arrested in Bangkok on March 6, Bout hired a battery of lawyers to fight extradition. The fight continued as this chapter was written. Meanwhile, the weapons Bout had sold around the world keep killing thousands every year.

2

Original Sins

Plymouth, Massachusetts

John Billington had been a problem from the day the *Mayflower* left England on its two-month voyage to the New World. He did not share the Pilgrim Separatist faith of the majority on board, who branded him a "knave" and "foul-mouthed miscreant."[1] In May 1621 he was convicted of contempt for insulting Captain Miles Standish, but he apologized to escape punishment. Three years later, Billington joined Reverend John Lyford in a plot to overthrow the government of Plymouth Colony. Lyford was banished, but the court allowed Billington to remain.

In September 1630 the troublemaker pushed his luck too far. While hunting deer, he met another colonist, John Newcomen, with whom he had recently quarreled. Still bearing a grudge, Billington shot Newcomen dead, and then blamed his victim for trespassing. Plymouth officials saw through the lie and convicted Billington of murder. Most historians regard his hanging as the first execution of a European settler in North America. Violence continued to haunt Billington's family. One of his descendants, President James Garfield, was assassinated by a deranged gunman in September 1881.

A HISTORY OF VIOLENCE

Concern with crime is as old as the human race. The first Bible stories after creation describe Eve stealing fruit from the tree of knowledge and

A carving of Hammurabi sits atop a pillar inscribed with the code of Hammurabi, which was established in 1760 B.C. *Art Media/HIP/ The Image Works*

Cain killing his brother Abel in a fit of jealousy. Every society on Earth has punished crime, from the Sumerian Code of Ur-Nammu (2100 B.C.) and Babylon's Code of Hammurabi (1760 B.C.) to the latest statutes on fraud and identity theft in the new cyberage.

Unfortunately, nothing seems to work.

Wherever humans go, crime follows. When ancient sailors ventured out to sea, they were pursued by pirates, a threat that persists in the 21st century. Chinese explored the uses of marijuana between 6000 and 4000 B.C., Mesopotamians began cultivating opium in 3400 B.C., and South Americans became addicted to coca leaves (from which cocaine is derived) around 3000 B.C. The first known victim of assassination was Gedaliah, governor of Judah (in present-day Israel), murdered in 586 B.C. The first identified serial killers practiced their gruesome hobby in

HEIDI FLEISS

Heidi Lynne Fleiss was born in Los Angeles on December 30, 1965, the daughter of an affluent physician and a school-teacher. As an adolescent she organized a babysitting service that employed her friends from school—and paid others to do her homework while she skipped class. Truancy prompted Fleiss to quit high school in her sophomore year, and by age 19 she was employed as personal secretary for international financier Bernard Cornfeld (1927-95). Fleiss doubled as Cornfeld's mistress, but his playboy lifestyle led to their breakup.

In 1987, while dating a Hollywood movie director, Fleiss met Elizabeth Adams, A.K.A. "Madam Alex," owner of an L.A. prostitution network serving celebrity clients. Facing legal problems at age 60, Adams hired Fleiss as a prostitute and soon promoted her to "assistant madam," managing most of the business. Profits quadrupled under Fleiss, and Heidi bought a $1.6 million mansion that she shared with best friend Victoria Sellers (daughter of actors Peter Sellers and Britt Ekland). Clients of the prostitution ring included Hollywood's top producers, directors, and stars such as Charlie Sheen.

Fleiss split from Madam Alex in 1991, in a dispute over profits, and launched her own service employing fashion models as prostitutes. Heidi's girls traveled as far afield as London and Paris, reportedly being paid $1,500 to $1 million from various wealthy clients. In 1992 Fleiss bought a second

ancient Rome, in 331 B.C. We owe the term "vandalism" to the Vandals, a Germanic tribe that looted Rome in A.D. 455.

Times change, but crime endures.

Five hundred years before Christopher Columbus "discovered" the New World, Vikings led by Leif Ericson planted small settlements in Vinland (now Newfoundland, Canada). One of Leif's sisters, Freydís Eiríksdóttir, quarreled with fellow colonists and falsely told her husband that two of the men tried to rape her. Enraged, her husband killed the pair and their friends while they slept, but he spared five women

L.A. home, but her notoriety betrayed her. In 1993, FBI agents joined Beverly Hills police and the Los Angeles County Sheriff's Department in a sting operation targeting Fleiss. Posing as a foreign businessman, an undercover officer arranged a party where Fleiss and four of her top girls were arrested on June 8, while in possession of 13 grams of cocaine.

Prosecutors charged Fleiss with various crimes, including narcotics possession and pandering (promoting prostitution). Local jurors convicted her of pandering in December 1994, resulting in a three-year prison sentence. A separate federal jury also convicted Fleiss of conspiracy, money laundering, and tax evasion in August 1995, producing another three-year sentence. Fleiss completed her California sentence in September 1996, and was paroled from federal custody in September 1999.

Controversy continues to dog Heidi Fleiss. Despite occasional legitimate employment with the Fox News network, as a columnist for *Maxim* magazine, and dispensing sex advice via the Internet, Fleiss remains a lightning rod for controversy and legal problems. In 2003 she accused her then-boyfriend, actor Tom Sizemore, of domestic violence, resulting in his criminal conviction. Her plans for a Nevada "stud farm" never materialized, but Fleiss opened a Laundromat called Dirty Laundry in the small desert town of Pahrump. In February 2008 police in Pahrump charged Fleiss with illegal possession of prescription drugs and driving under the influence.

from the rival group. Freydís then seized an axe and killed the women herself.

North America's oldest surviving city—St. Augustine, Florida—stands on the site where Spanish troops slaughtered French settlers in 1565. Three decades later, British pirate Sir Francis Drake attacked and burned the city. Spaniards rebuilt St. Augustine, but other pirates looted the city and killed most of its residents in 1688. Rebuilt again, it survived British attacks in 1702 and 1740, remaining today as a monument to endurance in the face of violence.

Meanwhile, the British colonies in North America suffered racial and religious warfare, smuggled contraband, dodged taxes, staged witch trials, and alternately battled or supported pirates. Then, as now, no one was safe from crime.

NEW WORLD DISORDER

While most historians downplay the fact, some of America's most honored founding fathers were involved in criminal or questionable activity. John Hancock, famed for his signature on the Declaration of Independence, was a wealthy smuggler before the American Revolution. John Adams, second president of the United States, led the violent Sons of Liberty, condemned as terrorists in 1772-75 for burning British ships and destroying their cargo. Alexander Hamilton, co-author of the *Federalist Papers* and America's first Secretary of the Treasury, employed corrupt aides whose thieving caused the country's first financial panic in 1792. Twelve years later, Vice President Aaron Burr killed Hamilton in a pistol duel.

Despite its new democracy, America remained a violent nation. Ignoring foreign wars, taxpayers' rebellions, and Indian battles, American courts executed at least 2,610 prisoners between July 1776 and the start of the Civil War in April 1861. Private "vigilance committees" lynched at least 202 suspected criminals during the same period, while an estimated 117 law enforcement officers died in the line of duty between 1792 and 1861.[2] No nationwide tally of murders exists for the 18th or 19th centuries.

A HOUSE DIVIDED

Predictably, the Civil War made matters worse. An estimated 618,222 military men lost their lives between 1861 and 1865, while civilian deaths topped 50,000.[3] Reconstruction brought peace to the North, but none in Dixie, where the Ku Klux Klan and similar groups behaved as if the war was still in progress. Between 1867 and 1876, white terrorists killed thousands of former slaves and whites who supported their claim to full civil rights, wounding or whipping thousands more. Again, no final tally is available, but Louisiana racists murdered 1,081 victims between April and October 1868 alone.[4]

While southern whites returned newly freed African Americans to a state of virtual slavery, wealthy political bosses and "robber barons" plundered the North and West. In New York City, Tammany Hall's political machine grew fat on graft while using street gangs to rig elections. Financiers James Fisk and Jay Gould bribed aides of President Ulysses Grant and sparked the "Black Friday" financial panic of 1869 by manipulating gold prices. Railroad tycoons linked the East and West Coasts, while grabbing huge tracts of land and bankrupting farmers with rigged shipping fees. Throughout the country, manufacturers and mine owners hired private armies to crush labor unions that sought higher wages and safer working conditions.

On the nation's frontiers, restless veterans of the Civil War found killing a difficult habit to break. Missouri's James and Younger brothers learned to rob trains as Confederate guerrillas, and in 1866 they "invented" daylight bank robbery. Indiana's Reno brothers deserted from the Union army to rob trains in the Midwest, continuing until they were lynched by vigilantes in 1868. Other notorious gangs—like the Dalton brothers, cousins of the Youngers—were also family affairs. Survivors and descendants carried on with robbery and kidnapping into the 1930s.

DRYING UP AMERICA

Sometimes the best intentions go awry, creating unimagined problems. America's temperance movement had lobbied for a ban on liquor from Colonial times, gaining momentum with creation of the Anti-Saloon League in 1895. Prohibition advanced by stages, starting with Maine's booze ban in 1851. Five other states went "dry" between 1880 and 1908, and 22 more joined the club during 1914–18.[5] The Eighteenth Amendment to the U.S. Constitution banned liquor nationwide in January 1920—and ushered in an era of unprecedented lawlessness.

SALEM WITCH TRIALS

Witch fever seized Boston, Massachusetts, in the summer of 1688, when five children of the Goodwin family experienced a rash of seizures lasting several weeks. Under coaching from their minister, Reverend Cotton Mather, the children accused their family's housekeeper—a Catholic indentured servant, "Goody" Glover—of bewitching them. Mather presided at Glover's trial, which resulted in her hanging, then published a booklet describing symptoms of demonic possession.

A year after Glover's execution, in November 1689, Rev. Samuel Parris moved from Boston to Salem as minister of the local Puritan church. He proved to be unpopular, and church members voted to cut off his salary in October 1691, but Parris remained in Salem. Three months later, nine-year-old Betty Parris and two young relatives suffered "fits" like those of the Goodwin children. Rev. Parris saw a chance to save his job by blaming witches, whereupon the girls accused a black slave named Tituba of enchanting them.

More accusations followed, as other children displayed signs of "possession." By year's end, more than 150 suspects were arrested and 29 of those were sentenced to die for witchcraft. Of the condemned, 19—including 14 women and five men—were actually hanged. (Unlike Europe, no witches were burned in America.) Five other defendants died in prison, and elderly farmer Giles Corey was crushed to death with stones in an effort to make him confess. Accused witches had better luck outside Salem, as 31 trials in Boston, Charlestown, and elsewhere produced only three convictions.

The Salem witch-hunt began losing steam on October 3, 1692, when Cotton Mather and his son, Rev. Increase Mather, publicly denounced the use of spectral evidence (unsup-

Supporters called Prohibition a "noble experiment." It was also a tragic failure.

The ban took effect at midnight on January 16, and Chicago gunmen staged the first liquor hijacking less than one hour later. New

ported accusations by self-proclaimed victims) to convict witchcraft defendants. Five days later, Massachusetts Governor William Phipps banned any further arrests, dissolved Salem's witch court, and released the defendants who had not been tried. In January 1693, 49 of those still imprisoned were freed on grounds that they were jailed solely on invalid spectral evidence. Members of Samuel Parris's church filed charges against him for his role in the witch trials, but he escaped punishment with an apology and remained in Salem until 1697, then moved on to serve other churches until his death in 1720.

Salem was not the first or only North American town to suffer from a witch craze. Between 1622 and 1688, at least 110 persons were accused of witchcraft in Connecticut, Maryland, Massachusetts, New Hampshire, New Mexico, Pennsylvania, and Virginia. Of those, 23 were hanged, 46 were whipped, and four were banished from their homes. After the Salem panic, another 20 witch trials were held between 1694 and 1762, in Connecticut, Maryland, New Jersey, New Mexico, South Carolina, and Virginia. All but one defendant—a New Mexico resident convicted and sold into slavery—were acquitted. Despite verdicts of innocence in court, two Connecticut women still were excommunicated from their church.[6]

Fear of witches seems childish today, but it lingers in various parts of the world. In April 2008, angry mobs in the Democratic Republic of the Congo attacked 13 alleged sorcerers accused of using black magic to steal male genitalia. Police jailed the victims for their own protection. In May 2008, residents of western Kenya lynched 11 elderly women suspected of witchcraft. Two months later, a mob at Mananga, South Africa, attacked a 77-year-old man accused of shape-shifting to become a baboon.

York City had 15,000 licensed saloons before 1920, and at least 32,000 outlaw "speakeasies" afterward. Nationwide, government spokesmen estimated that 500,000 illegal bars served thirsty customers, supplied by smugglers, alcohol stolen from government storage, plus thousands of illegal breweries and distilleries.[7] Most of the speakeasies also provided gambling and prostitution. Former small-time gangsters became millionaires overnight, bribing police and judges to ignore their crimes.

Easy money prompted gang wars to control the traffic in illegal alcohol. While no nationwide death statistics exist, it is known that at least 689 gangsters were killed in Chicago alone, between 1920 and 1933. The government claimed 512 Prohibition officers slain by bootleggers, and admitted killing 2,089 liquor violators. Critics suspected that the civilian death toll was much higher, and Agent Clarence Pickering alone admitted killing 42 alleged smugglers along the Canadian border. Most of those were unarmed, shot down while "resisting arrest."[8] Eventually, bad publicity from all the killing prompted gangsters to cooperate more peacefully, forming a national crime syndicate that still exists today.

The worst effect of Prohibition was the government corruption it encouraged. President Warren Harding served bootleg liquor to guests at the White House. Detroit, with only 129 positions for customs agents assigned to catch smugglers, saw 175 agents fired in one year for accepting payoffs, indicating the high turnover due to corruption. Ohio's state treasurer and prohibition director were jailed for protecting bootleggers. Chicago police chief William Fitzmorris told reporters that 50 percent of his officers were "involved seriously" in liquor violations. Nationwide, the U.S. Prohibition Bureau hired 17,816 agents between 1920 and 1930—and fired 13,513 of them for misconduct.[9]

Despite those drawbacks, the government *did* try to enforce Prohibition. From 1920 to 1930, federal agents arrested some 577,000 offenders and convicted 343,000, collecting almost $57 million in fines. They raided 1.6 million stills, large and small, seizing more than 2 billion gallons of illegal alcohol, plus 45,000 cars and 1,300 boats, all valued in excess of $49 million. The price of federal enforcement efforts topped $36 billion—$10 billion more than the cost of U.S. involvement in World War I.[10] No statistics for state arrests and seizures were compiled.

Prohibition was repealed by the Twenty-first Amendment in December 1933, after 14 years of violence and futile efforts to dry up the nation. Few major bootleggers were jailed for selling liquor or killing their rivals, but a handful were convicted of evading income taxes. Most smoothly shifted their focus to other crimes such as gambling, prostitution, labor racketeering, and narcotics trafficking. The corruption spawned by Prohibition worsened through the 1930s and beyond, affecting government at every level.

Prohibition illustrates the inherent difficulty of punishing consensual crimes, mirrored today by laws banning gambling, prostitution, and various drugs. No statute passed in history has curbed public demand for "sinful" pleasures, and criminals who furnish outlawed substances or services continue to corrupt police and politicians worldwide. American police seized 11,412,861 pounds of illegal drugs during 2000-03, without putting a dent in the traffic. In 2007 alone, 1,841,200 Americans were arrested for drug violations. In December 2006, American prisons held 4,237,023 inmates, of whom 8 percent (342,298) were jailed for drug offenses.[11]

Critics of victimless crime prosecutions condemn such laws as costly relics of a bygone age. They note the expense of keeping drug offenders in prison—more than $7.2 billion in 2006 alone—and suggest that money should be spent pursuing violent criminals or white-collar thieves. [12] Proponents of legalization also noted that 12 states with legalized casinos collected more than $5.6 billion in gambling taxes during 2008, while eliminating the expense of arresting and prosecuting gamblers.[13]

The same economic argument is raised by those who support legalizing prostitution. Nevada is the only U.S. state that permits prostitution (in counties with fewer than 400,000 residents), and while the state has no income tax, it collected business and license fees from 30 brothels in 2008. County fees range from $200 to $100,000 per brothel, and some counties earn 25 percent of their business fees from prostitution. Lyon County, with a single brothel, collected $341,000 in 2007. In 2005 brothel owners asked the state to impose a business tax of two dollars per customer, thus raising an estimated $3.2 million for schools in 2006-07, but lawmakers rejected the proposal.[14]

Various foreign countries collect sizable tax revenue from licensed brothels. In Antwerp, Belgium—a city of 500,000—brothels pay an average $800,000 in taxes each year. Since prostitution was legalized in 2001, Belgian police report that crimes including murder, rape, assault, drug trafficking, and vandalism have declined by 44 percent. In Britain, during 2001, the Royal Economic Society reported that legalizing prostitution would raise £770 million ($1.2 billion) per year in taxes, but Parliament refused to support the plan.[15]

Opponents of dropping the ban on consensual crimes raise two separate but related arguments. The first, based chiefly on religious principles, condemns the prohibited acts as "immoral." The second, used long ago to support prohibition of liquor, contends that banned activities and substances damage society, luring minors to sample supposed "adult" pleasures, and disrupting families or leaving them bankrupt where parents waste their money on gambling, drugs, and so forth. Statistics on teenage drinking and smoking suggest that some of those fears, at least, may be well-founded, but modern lawmakers have not seen fit to ban alcohol or tobacco.

Negative effects of gambling include the obvious loss of money by players and the spread of other crimes related to casinos: rigged games of chance, tax-evasion through "skimming" of profits, loan-sharking by organized crime, and proliferation of other consensual crimes— prostitution, drug use, and heavy drinking—commonly associated with gambling. Prostitution, likewise, may spread serious diseases and contribute to violent crimes, including robbery of "johns" and assault or murder of streetwalkers. While reliable statistics are sparse, a 1994 survey of Minneapolis prostitutes found that 85 percent had contracted diseases from their clients, 23 percent had suffered broken bones from customer assaults, and 90 percent had endured domestic violence at home.[16] Various surveys also estimate that illegal drugs claim an average 17,000 lives per year in America, compared to 435,000 killed by tobacco and 85,000 deaths related to alcohol.[17]

The debate continues, with no end in sight.

Crimes of Violence

Blacksburg, Virginia

Seung-Hui Cho was a troubled young man. At age three, in his native South Korea, he had been so shy that relatives suspected he was an autistic mute. They were mistaken, but he grew up suffering from clinical depression, harassed by bullies who mocked his speech impediment. When he came to the United States and enrolled at Virginia Polytechnical Institute and State University, administrators there were not informed of his background. They soon realized that Cho had problems, however. He disrupted classes and was charged with stalking female students. In 2005 a judge declared Cho mentally ill and ordered him to seek psychiatric treatment.

Instead, he started buying guns.

On April 18, 2007, Cho scrawled a suicide note denouncing the "rich kids" and "debauchery" at Virginia Tech, then went on a shooting rampage across campus, killing 32 victims and wounding 17 others before he shot himself. Cho's rampage was the worst mass murder in American history, surpassing the previous record of 23 killed and 20 wounded by Texas gunman George Hennard in 1991.

AMERICA THE VIOLENT

When politicians talk about restoring "law and order," they are normally referring to the violent crimes that frighten average Americans at home, at work, and on the streets. And based on crime statistics gathered by the FBI, that fear is not unfounded. Between 2003 and 2007 American police recorded 83,375 murders, 466,503 forcible rapes, and 2,125,671 robberies.[1] Even though most of the country's 305 million residents suffer no personal attacks in any given year, many know someone who *has* been victimized, and media reports of brutal crimes contribute to a siege mentality that amplifies the national crime problem.

Few crimes are more sensational than multiple murders, committed without any rational motive. It can be understood, without condoning

ST. VALENTINE'S DAY MASSACRE

The most notorious gangland slaying of the Prohibition era occurred in Chicago on February 14, 1929—St. Valentine's Day—when gunmen disguised as police killed seven men in a garage on North Clark Street. The massacre climaxed five years of warfare between Al Capone's gang and North Side rivals led successively by Dion O'Bannion, Earl Weiss, and George "Bugs" Moran. O'Bannion was murdered in his flower shop on November 10, 1924, and Weiss was shot from ambush with four fellow gangsters on October 12, 1926, but Moran carried on the fight until Capone and his chief triggerman, Vincenzo Gibaldi (alias "Machine Gun" Jack McGurn) decided to wipe out the North Side Gang's leadership, once and for all.

The trap was set with aid from Detroit's Purple Gang, which offered Moran a truckload of hijacked whiskey, scheduled for delivery to his garage at 10:30 A.M. on February 14. Two members of the Purple Gang rented an apartment nearby, watching men arrive at the garage, and telephoned Capone's gang when they thought Moran was inside.

But they were wrong.

In fact, the man they mistook for Moran was Al Weinshank, who ran one of Moran's saloons. The others present were brothers Frank and Peter Gusenberg, who had wounded Gibaldi in 1928; Albert Kashellek, Moran's brother-in-law; bookkeeper Adam Heyer; John May, the gang's mechanic; and Dr. Reinhart Schwimmer, an optometrist who moonlighted

it, when criminals kill one another, but the random acts of individuals who kill and kill again evoke extreme reactions, sometimes verging on panic.

The FBI recognizes six kinds of murder, based on the number of victims. *Single, double,* and *triple* murders are self-explanatory. *Mass murder*—like the slaughter at Virginia Tech—is defined as any slaying of four or more victims in a single event. The FBI defines *spree murder* as the killing of three or more victims at different places, in one ongoing

in bootlegging. All were surprised when four "policemen" entered the garage at 10:30, pretending to conduct a liquor raid. When Moran's men were disarmed and lined against a wall, the intruders opened fire at close range with machine guns and shotguns.

No one was ever prosecuted for the massacre. Al Capone was in Florida when it happened, and Gibaldi/McGurn had an airtight alibi. The killers' car was found a week later, partially burned in a Chicago garage, but it furnished no clues. A break of sorts occurred in March 1931, when Michigan authorities arrested St. Louis gangster Fred "Killer" Burke for shooting a policeman in December 1929. In his possession, officers found loot from a Wisconsin bank robbery and two machine guns used in the St. Valentine's Day massacre. Despite that circumstantial evidence, Burke was never tried for the Chicago crime. Convicted of the policeman's murder, he received a life sentence and died in prison on July 10, 1940.

By that time, Capone was serving time for tax evasion and Gibaldi was long dead, gunned down in a Chicago bowling alley on February 13, 1936. His unknown killers left a greeting card that read:

You've lost your job
You've lost your dough
Your jewels and handsome houses.
But things could be worse, you know.
You haven't lost your trousers.[2]

event. Finally, *serial murder*—like the crimes of Theodore Bundy—is defined as the killing of three or more victims at different locations, with an "emotional cooling-off period" between murders.[3]

The FBI's classification system has certain defects. First, there seems to be no clear reason for separating mass and spree murder. The bureau's prime example of "spree" killing is New Jersey gunman Howard Unruh, who shot 16 victims within 20 minutes, while strolling around his home neighborhood. While the FBI insists that Unruh's crime "was not classified as a mass murder because he moved to different locations," media reports of the event in 1949 *did* use that term, and the FBI's distinction was not proposed until 1988.[4] Likewise, the official definition of serial murder ignores slayers like Jeffrey Dahmer and John Gacy, who kill most of their victims at one location, and it offers no label for repeat slayers who are captured after their second murder.

Serial killers are the rarest of criminals, but America claims more than its share. While the trend remains unexplained, 80 percent of all serial slayers identified during the twentieth century were found in the United States. The worst five states for serial murder, ranked by number of cases recorded, were California (with nearly 10 percent of the *world* total), Florida, New York, Texas, and Illinois.[5] No comparable statistics exist for mass murder, but easy access to firearms increases the potential for tragic killing sprees.

GUNS AND CRIME

America recorded 16,929 murders in 2007, with 10,086 of those victims (59.6 percent) slain by firearms. Of the 32,637 suicides reported nationwide in 2005, 17,002 (52.1 percent) were committed with guns. Estimates of yearly accidental deaths from gunshots vary. In 2000, 97,300 Americans died from accidental injuries, 600 of them firearms accidents (including 80 children age 14 or younger). The following year, there were 802 fatal accidents involving guns. One source estimates that nonfatal shooting accidents average 200,000 per year nationwide.[6]

The U.S. Constitution's Second Amendment reads: "A well regulated militia being necessary to the security of a free State, the right of the People to keep and bear arms shall not be infringed." But despite its apparent simplicity, that rule has inspired heated controversy spanning three centuries.

At the extremes, some pro-gun advocates believe that virtually anyone is entitled to own any firearm, including military-style weapons, while their zealous opponents would ban guns completely. More moderate debate concerns the Second Amendment's reference to "a well regulated militia," with critics (and some courts) contending that the Constitution's authors sought to arm a military force—known today as the National Guard.

Despite the Second Amendment's wording, the right of private citizens to keep and "bear" (carry) weapons *has* been infringed repeatedly, throughout history. The National Rifle Association claims that some 20,000 local, state and federal gun-control laws presently exist in the United States.[7] Many other laws restrict or ban possession of other weapons, including various knives, clubs, brass knuckles, and explosives.

Six federal laws concerning firearms affect the Second Amendment rights of all Americans. They include:

o The National Firearms Act of 1934, which restricted (but did not ban) private ownership of "gangster" weapons such as machine guns, sawed-off shotguns or rifles, and firearm "silencers."

o The Omnibus Crime Control and Safe Streets Act of 1968, banning interstate traffic in guns except between licensed dealers, and fixed the minimum age for ownership of pistols at 21.

o The Gun Control Act of 1968, banning possession of firearms by various persons, including convicted or indicted felons, fugitives from justice, drug addicts, persons judged mentally ill, illegal aliens, those dishonorably discharged from the military, persons who renounce their U.S. citizenship, anyone subject to restraining orders for stalking or domestic violence, and those below age 18.

o The Firearms Owners Protection Act of 1986, which relaxed some of the restrictions of the Gun Control Act of 1968, while banning private possession of machine guns manufactured after May 1986.

o The Brady Handgun Violence Prevention Act of 1993, which required a waiting period for background checks before purchase

of a pistol. The delay was theoretically eliminated by establishment of the FBI's National Instant Criminal Background Check System, but that online network failed to prevent Seung-Hui Cho from acquiring pistols in Virginia.
o The Gun Control Act of 2008, which imposed no new restrictions but earmarked $1.3 billion to improve state tracking of persons forbidden to own firearms.

Gun control remains a "hot button" topic in America, where anti-gun forces suggest that the founding fathers never visualized a crowded nation without wild frontiers, where professional law enforcement limits the need for armed self-defense. Pro-gun spokesmen offer contradictory statistics indicating that somewhere between 108,000 and 2.5 million Americans use guns to defend themselves from criminals each year.[8]

COLLECTIVE VIOLENCE

Individual assaults and murders are frightening enough. Worse still are incidents wherein large crowds or whole communities join in a violent frenzy of attacks on property and human beings. Armed rebellions, riots, and lynchings represent the most radical departure from a so-called civilized society.

Some Americans disliked the government established by the Constitution so intensely that they took up arms against it. Taxes triggered Shays' Rebellion in Massachusetts (1786) and Pennsylvania's Whiskey Rebellion (1794), while dissatisfaction with Rhode Island's voting procedures sparked the Dorr Rebellion of 1841-42. Eleven southern states left the Union during 1860-61, in defense of slavery, but they lost the war that followed and the Supreme Court's 1869 decision in *Texas v. White* proclaimed that states have no right to secede. Armed rebellions against Washington ended there, until 1983, when the racist Silent Brotherhood declared war on the federal government. Their brief campaign, which never rose to the scale of earlier rebellions, ended with all known members of the group dead or in prison.

Riots are more common in America, with hundreds recorded since Boston's Bread Riot of 1713, leaving thousands dead and tens out of thousands injured. Such outbreaks may be spontaneous (like the vio-

Two youths with lampshades looted from a store run down a street in the Watts section of Los Angeles during the Watts Riots. *AP Photo*

lence that rocked 125 cities after the 1968 assassination of Dr. Martin Luther King Jr.), or carefully planned in advance by conspirators (as in the anti-Catholic "Know-Nothing" riots of the 1840s and Ku Klux Klan riots against "freedom riders" in 1961). While riots often seem to grow from minor incidents—such as the arrest of a drunk driver which sparked the Los Angeles Watts riot of 1965—closer investigation commonly reveals months or years of unrest preceding the final explosion.

Lynching—named for Virginia "hanging judge" Charles Lynch (1736-96)—is illegal execution by a mob, often targeting persons accused of some crime.[9] Unofficial "vigilance committees" killed hundreds of suspected thieves, gamblers, and other lawbreakers across the country, but lynching is most infamous for its use in the South as a means of terrorizing African Americans, who might have been tortured and killed at the whim of white racists for "offenses" such as arguing with whites or refusing to sell real estate on demand. Lynching statistics vary, depending on the source consulted. No tally exists before 1882, when Alabama's Tuskegee Institute began keeping detailed records, reporting 4,733 lynchings by 1959. In those cases, 3,437 victims were black, while 1,293 were white. Conflicting sources online claim 4,743 lynchings between 1882 and 1968, or "more than 6,000" between 1865 and 1965.[10]

PRIVATE ARMIES

Corporate employment of armed security forces—private armies, in effect—has a long history in the United States. Agents of the Pinkerton Detective Agency, formed in 1850, often served as strikebreakers for management until the Homestead Strike of 1892, against Pennsylvania's Carnegie Steel Company, ended with a battle between Pinkertons and strikers that left 16 persons dead. Another Pennsylvania institution, the Coal and Iron Police, served mining companies from 1865 until 1902. Its private officers were frequently accused of violent crimes, including murders of union members, but none were ever brought to trial.

Today, such groups have been replaced by private military companies, employed by governments around the world for jobs where use of tax-supported soldiers might be controversial or reduce efficiency of military units in the field. In recent years, such groups have guarded politicians and corporate officers, battled drug cartels, and trained native security forces from Eastern Europe to Africa, the Middle East, and Taiwan. The industry generates more than $100 billion in revenue per year.[11] Predictably, that mercenary gold rush has spawned controversy.

In February 2006 a sniper employed by North Carolina-based Blackwater Worldwide killed three Iraqi security

ORGANIZED VIOLENCE

Random eruptions of mayhem are frightening and destructive, but they rarely pose any long-term threat to society. The same cannot be said for crimes committed by organized groups that use violence in pursuit of profit or some other agenda. The gangs or syndicates which fall into that category frequently defy police attempts to infiltrate and prosecute them.

While the term *gang* may refer to any group of people sharing a common identity or goal, in modern times it generally describes criminal organizations. Street gangs, the most common form, are urban

---

guards outside the Justice Ministry in Baghdad.[12] Police reports called the shooting "an act of terrorism" committed "without any provocation."[13] The U.S. State Department disagreed, accepting Blackwater's claims that the government employees shot first, announcing that the sniper's action "fell within approved rules governing the use of force."[14]

On Christmas Eve 2006 a drunken Blackwater agent shot and killed a bodyguard of Iraq's vice president. Blackwater fired the gunman for "violating alcohol and firearm policy," but State Department officials concealed his identity, and Combat Support Associates hired him in August 2007 to work for the U.S. Department of Defense in Kuwait.[15]

In September 2007, Blackwater employees killed 17 Iraqis in Baghdad, at least 14 of them shot "without cause," according to the FBI. State Department spokesmen admitted that "innocent life was lost," yet they granted the Blackwater gunmen immunity from prosecution in October. As a result, Iraq banned Blackwater from any further operations in the country.

In November 2008, the State Department slapped Blackwater with a multimillion-dollar fine for shipping hundreds of guns to Iraq without proper permits. Some of the weapons allegedly were sold to terrorists on the country's black market.[16]

groups of relatively young people engaged in various crimes. Originally formed in self-defense against enemies from other neighborhoods or ethnic groups, street gangs evolved by the mid-19th century into groups of organized thieves and extortionists, often allied with big-city political bosses. Today conflicts among rival gangs continue, and many street gangs are involved with illegal activities such as drug trafficking and prostitution. In 2000 the Department of Justice counted more than 24,500 street gangs nationwide, with membership exceeding 772,500.[17]

While street gangs have always been violent to some extent, participation in drug trafficking has greatly increased the number of gang-related murders in America. According to the National Criminal Justice Reference Center, such killings escalated from 580 nationwide in 1999, to 819 in 2003.[18] Few other national statistics are available, but the Los Angeles Police Department (LAPD) publishes detailed information on gang violence in Los Angeles. During the first six months of 2009, L.A. gang members committed 74 murders, 1,268 aggravated assaults, 33 attacks on police, 14 reported rapes, 1,054 robberies, 40 carjackings, 19 kidnappings, 84 drive-by shootings at homes, and one arson.[19]

Another class of gangs is formed in prisons then spread to the outside world as members are released from custody. Such gangs—known to prison administrators as "security threat groups"—generally choose their members based on race and willingness to commit violent acts on command. They battle gangs of other races, assault or kill prison guards, and deal drugs on both sides of prison walls. Some perform contract murders for profit and engage in other crimes outside of prison. At present, the FBI recognizes 13 major American prison gangs, dominated by the Aryan Brotherhood, Black Guerrilla Family, Mexican Mafia, and Nuestra Familia ("Our Family").[20]

Outlaw motorcycle gangs began in the United States and later spread worldwide, with chapters found today from Canada to Europe and Australia. The FBI recognizes more than 300 biker gangs in America, ranging from tiny groups with five or six members to the dominant "Big Four": the Hells Angels, Outlaws, Bandidos, and Pagans. Common motorcycle gang activities are drug-smuggling (with emphasis on methamphetamines), gun-running, and prostitution. Turf wars between major rivals have claimed hundreds of lives nationwide and around the world since the 1970s. In Québec, a war between Hells Angels and Mongols produced 150 murders in the 1990s. In Scandinavia, between 1994 and 1997, Bandidos and Hells Angels fought the "Great Nordic Biker War," killing 11 persons, wounding 96, and committing at least 74 attempted murders.[21]

When organized crime is mentioned, most Americans think of the Mafia, which restricts its membership to persons of Sicilian heritage. That attitude, spawned by informants in the 1960s and the later series of *Godfather* novels and films, sometimes attributes any organized criminal activity to Italian conspirators, but while the Mafia exists, it is neither the oldest nor the largest oath-bound criminal organization. No record exists of the "Mafia" name being used before 1863, whereas China's Triad societies date from 1644 and Japan's Yakuza trace their roots to the Genroku Era (1688-1704). With an estimated 3,000 members in America and some 20,000 in Europe, the Mafia is dwarfed by the Yakuza (110,000 members), Triads (80,000 alone in the largest of 10 recognized gangs), and Russian syndicates (100,000 to 300,000).[22]

While members of organized crime are less violent today than during Prohibition, they still settle disputes with bloodshed. The FBI recorded 190 apparent gangland murders, credited to killers involved in "traditional" organized crime, during 2002 and 2003.[23] Most of those slain were gangsters themselves or directly involved in criminal activity, but such is not always the case. In Sicily, home of the Mafia, or in Colombia and Mexico, where drug cartels comprise a kind of shadow government, common targets include police, public officials, and reporters. In November 1985, political extremists hired by rich drug dealers fearing extradition to America invaded the Palace of Justice in Bogotá, killed 11 Supreme Court judges, and destroyed vital criminal records. When police stormed the building, more than 100 others died, including hostages, government employees, and all of the guerrillas.

Some violent criminal groups are driven by motives other than profit, including racism and extreme religious or political beliefs. The Ku Klux Klan has murdered thousands since its creation in 1866, and members were still fighting racial progress in the 1960s, bombing hundreds of schools, churches, homes, and other targets on both sides of the Mason-Dixon line. In the early 1970s, opponents of the war in

Vietnam turned to bombing as a means of protest, while certain "pro-life" Christians did the same a decade later, blasting women's clinics and shooting abortion providers. Prior to the deadly skyjackings of September 2001, the worst terrorist attack on American soil was the 1995 bombing of a federal building in Oklahoma City, which claimed 168 lives. Today, the FBI issues stern warnings against "eco-terrorists" who sabotage logging operations and otherwise harass those whom they say endanger the environment.

As demonstrated throughout history, one person's terrorist may be another's hero.

Drugs
and Crime

Washington, D.C.
On September 17, 2008, Attorney General Michael Mukasey announced the arrest of 175 narcotics smugglers in the United States and Italy. The raids were part of "Project Reckoning," a campaign involving the Drug Enforcement Administration (DEA), Italian police, and Mexican authorities. Since 2007, Project Reckoning had produced 507 arrests, plus seizures including $60.1 million in cash; 51,258 pounds of marijuana; 36,764 pounds of cocaine; 1,039 pounds of methamphetamine; 19 pounds of heroin; 176 vehicles; and 167 weapons.[1]

Project Reckoning targets Mexico's Gulf Cartel, a drug-trafficking network that ships illegal drugs from Mexico, Colombia, Guatemala, and Panama. While the cartel remains in business, Italian prosecutor Nicola Gratteri told reporters, "This operation exemplifies the European vision of the international fight against drug trafficking."[2]

HISTORICAL HIGHS

Drugs derived from natural sources have entertained and troubled societies throughout history. Chinese cooks were using cannabis (hemp/ marijuana) seeds in recipes by 6000 B.C., and Chinese physicians began treating patients with cannabis around 2727 B.C. Ancient Sumerians cultivated opium poppies from 3400 B.C. onward, and the crop found its way to Egypt by 1300 B.C. South American natives discovered the pleasures of chewing coca leaves by 3000 B.C. The "harder" drugs came

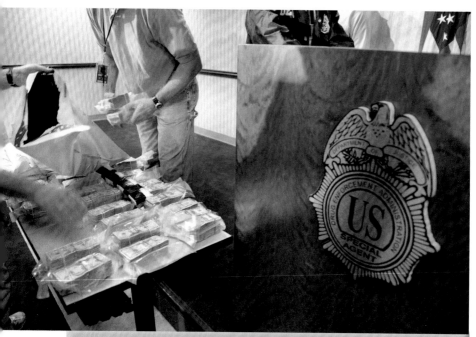

Drug Enforcement Administration agents pack up cash in Atlanta, Georgia on September 17, 2008. The money was confiscated as a part of Project Reckoning, a multi-agency, law-enforcement effort targeting the Mexican, drug-trafficking organization known as the Gulf Cartel. *AP Photo/The Journal & Constitution/Joey Ivansco*

later: morphine and heroin derived from opium in 1803 and 1874, respectively, and cocaine isolated from coca in 1859.

Colonial pioneers would not recognize modern America's attitude toward cannabis. In 1619 England's Virginia Company ordered Jamestown colonists to cultivate at least 100 hemp plants each. Between 1662 and 1706, Virginia, Maryland, Connecticut, and Pennsylvania offered bounties for hemp production. American presidents George Washington and Thomas Jefferson were substantial hemp-growers, and Jefferson drafted the Declaration of Independence on paper made from cannabis fibers.

Unlike modern "drug wars," the first armed conflicts over drugs sprang from Britain's insistence that China import British opium. China banned opium imports in 1799, but British smugglers persisted. Finally, British armed forces fought two Opium Wars against China, in 1839–42

Alleged Gulf Cartel operator Juan Daniel Carranco Salazar is presented to the media in Mexico City after being arrested on August 10, 2009. *AP Photo*

and 1856–60, forcing China to accept large quantities of opium and to surrender ownership of Hong Kong.

America's best-selling soft drink, Coca-Cola, was invented in 1886. Its main ingredients were cocaine and caffeine from kola nuts. The

HARRY ANSLINGER (1892–1975)

America owes much of its present drug policy to Harry Anslinger, who credited his hard-line attitudes to childhood observation of drug addicts in Altoona, Pennsylvania. In 1917 he married a niece of Andrew Mellon (1855-1937), who served as Secretary of the Treasury from 1921 to 1932. Soon after taking office, Mellon hired Anslinger as an assistant commissioner in the Bureau of Prohibition, and then appointed him to lead the new Federal Bureau of Narcotics in 1930. Anslinger retained that office until 1962, nearly rivaling the reign of FBI Director J. Edgar Hoover.

Anslinger hated drugs, drug dealers, and drug addicts. Marijuana was his particular focus until 1937, when Congress passed the Marijuana Tax Act based primarily on propaganda generated by the FBN, including films like *Reefer Madness* (1936), deemed laughable today for their portrayal of dangerous behavior by cannabis users. Most scientists reject Anslinger's portrayal of marijuana as a source of "brainwashing" and violence, though debate continues regarding its role as a "gateway drug" leading to use of narcotics.

On a more positive note, Anslinger recognized the role of organized crime in international drug-trafficking 30 years before J. Edgar Hoover admitted the existence of a national crime syndicate. In 1950, when Hoover refused to assist Senator Estes Kefauver's investigation of interstate gambling, Anslinger opened his files in full cooperation. Anslinger retired from the FBN at age 70, suffering from a decline in health that left him blind by 1973. He died from heart failure in 1975, at a hospital in his native Altoona.

original recipe included five ounces of coca leaf per gallon of syrup—or nine milligrams of cocaine per glass. The cocaine was removed in 1903, but Coke still features coca flavoring.

Opium was even more popular. During America's Civil War, Union doctors dispensed 175,000 pounds of opium powder and 500,000 opium pills to wounded soldiers. After the war, some 200,000 U.S. addicts got their "fix" from 50,000 patent medicines containing opium. By 1906, 13.5 million Chinese—27 percent of the adult male population—were opium addicts, consuming 39,000 tons yearly.[3]

THE LONGEST WAR

America's "war on drugs" spans 130-odd years. San Francisco banned opium dens in 1878 but still allowed importation. In 1909, the Smoking Opium Exclusion Act banned "smoking opium" but ignored opium-based medicines. The first broad restriction on opiates came in 1914, with passage of the Harrison Narcotic Act. In 1922 the Narcotic Drug Import and Export Act further restricted shipment of opium and coca. The Heroin Act of 1924 banned manufacture, importation, and possession of heroin.

In June 1930 the Federal Bureau of Narcotics (FBN) was created to enforce federal drug laws. Two years later, encouraged by FBN chief Harry Anslinger, Congress passed the Uniform State Narcotic Act, encouraging various states to ban marijuana. By 1937, when Congress passed the Marijuana Tax Act, imposing a one-dollar nuisance tax on cannabis sales, all 48 states had followed the FBN's lead.

The American drug war escalated during and after World War II. In 1942 the Opium Poppy Control Act banned possession or growing of opium poppies without a government license. In 1951 the Boggs Act lumped marijuana with narcotics and imposed sentences of two, five, and 10 years for successive offenses. Five years later, the Narcotic Control Act raised penalties to 10, 20, and 40 years for successive convictions, with a potential life sentence for heroin sales.

In 1968 the FBN became the Bureau of Narcotics and Dangerous Drugs, assigned to the Justice Department, then changed again in 1973, to become the Drug Enforcement Administration (DEA). By then, President Nixon had named drug abuse as "Public Enemy No. 1," but Watergate soon distracted him from the crusade. Jimmy Carter's 1976 presidential campaign included plans to decriminalize marijuana, but he soon abandoned the idea.[4]

President Reagan launched a new drug war in 1982, placing Vice President Bush in command of an anti-drug task force in southern Florida. Four years later, Reagan signed the Anti-Drug Abuse Act of 1986, creating mandatory minimum penalties for drug offenses. A second Anti-Drug Abuse Act, passed in 1988, allowed execution of "drug kingpins," but none have been condemned. In 1989, President Bush created the Office of Drug Control Policy and labeled its chief a "drug czar," although the Constitution forbids royal titles for government officials.[5]

WHAT WAR ON DRUGS?

The Reagan-Bush drug war accomplished little. Critics labeled it a war of words, noting that Attorney General William Smith concealed records of the Florida task force's activities, while Reagan's budget cuts put 19,609 federal agents out of work by December 1982. In June 1982 the Government Accounting Office found that street prices for heroin had dropped 74 percent since 1979, a sure sign that supplies were increasing. Speaking of the Bush task force in 1984, Florida congressman Claude Pepper told the *New York Times*, "I can't see a single thing it has accomplished." A Florida Coast Guard commander described the drug war as "an intellectual fraud."[6]

Worse yet, proof soon emerged that one federal agency had been actively involved in drug-trafficking for four decades.

President Harry Truman created the Central Intelligence Agency in July 1947, to protect America from foreign enemies. Two months later, the CIA forged its first alliance with drug-dealing gangsters, using the French Mafia to disrupt communist election campaigns in Marseilles. Those same gangsters ran the so-called French Connection, smuggling heroin into New York until 1972.[7]

In 1950 the CIA moved on to collaborate with the Taiwan government of former Chinese president Chiang Kai-shek (1887-1975), a longtime member of the Triad syndicate whose regime smuggled heroin from Asia aboard cargo planes owned by the CIA.[8]

After Fidel Castro seized control of Cuba, the CIA hired members of the Mafia to kill him. The gangsters were glad to oblige, since Castro had closed their Havana casinos, but a series of bungled attempts during 1960-63 left Castro unscathed. Mobsters also supported the 1961 Bay of Pigs invasion, which failed to topple Castro's government.[9]

The Vietnam War forged another CIA-heroin link, as Air America—the agency's charter airline—exported tons of opium from Burma and Laos between 1965 and 1976. Florida gangster Santo Trafficante Jr.—a participant in the anti-Castro plots—visited South Vietnam in 1968 to arrange drug shipments. During the same years, America's addict population reached 750,000.[10]

The Reagan-Bush era highlighted new enemies, but CIA tactics remained the same. After President Reagan ordered "destabilization" of Nicaragua's legally elected government, the CIA supported guerrilla attacks on Nicaraguan officials and civilians. Congress banned federal support for the rebels in 1984, but Reagan persisted, while the CIA raised funds by trafficking cocaine. The resultant scandal produced several convictions and guilty pleas, but President Bush pardoned most of those defendants in December 1992.[11]

Three years later, journalist Gary Webb published a series of articles linking the CIA to proliferation of crack cocaine in America, spawned by the war in Nicaragua. The agency "cleared" itself of any wrongdoing, while reluctantly admitting that some agents beyond its control may have sold drugs. Newspapers including the *New York Times, Washington Post*, and *Los Angeles Times* condemned Webb for spreading "paranoia" in urban ghettoes plagued by crack. In December 2004, Webb committed suicide with *two* gunshots to the head, according to a coroner's report.[12]

THE WAR HITS HOME

While politicians debate the war on drugs and law enforcement officers struggle to halt the traffic in controlled substances, illegal drugs have a severe impact on daily life in the United States. While statistics are sporadically reported, and are often subject to debate, they provide indications of the threat posed by illicit drugs.

The most severe of those is death. An estimated 3 million Americans had serious drug problems in 2004, all at risk for various life-threatening conditions. In 2000, researchers tabulated 17,000 drug-related deaths, including those from accidental overdoses, homicide, suicide, motor vehicle accidents, and a range of diseases including AIDS, hepatitis, and pneumonia.[13]

While many drug-law violators are imprisoned simply for possessing controlled substances, drug abuse also spawns other crimes. A survey of federal prison inmates, conducted in 2004, found that offenses committed specifically to obtain money for drugs included 14.8 percent of all violent crimes, 10.6 percent of property crimes, 25.3 percent of illegal drug sales, and 6.8 percent of public-order offenses (such as prostitution and illegal gambling).[14]

Violent crimes naturally cause the greatest concern. Between 1987 and 2007, a total of 18,782 Americans were murdered by offenders acting under the influence of drugs. A survey of workplace violence spanning the years from 1993 to 1999 found that 35 percent of all offenders were using drugs when their crimes occurred.[15] In Mexico, the current source of most illegal drugs consumed in the United States, drug-related violence claimed at least 13,274 lives between December 2006 and August 2009.[16]

While these statistics are admittedly incomplete and often subject to debate, they make a persuasive case that drug abuse is not simply a "victimless" crime.

RETHINKING PROHIBITION

Debate continues over the wisdom of banning various drugs and punishing those who use them. Authorities freely admit that most drugs smuggled into the country elude them, while the drug war's cost keeps climbing. Between January 1 and November 28, 2008, 1,721,427 drug offenders were jailed in America, at a cost of $46.2 billion. A new arrest occurs every 17 seconds, while the government spends $600 per second to stem the tide of drugs.[17]

Supporters of the drug war argue that no financial cost is too high, and that those arrested have only themselves to blame. They argue that drugs are "immoral," dangerous to users, and that they cause other crimes as addicts run amok or steal to support their habits.

In fact, some drugs *are* dangerous. Aside from addiction, health risks include birth defects, poisoning by contaminated drugs, potentially fatal infections from shared hypodermic needles, and accidental overdoses. Celebrity overdose victims make global headlines, but many other users die virtually unnoticed. According to the Centers for Disease Control (CDC), deaths from accidental overdoses in America increased from 11,155 in 1999 to 19,838 in 2004, with a majority caused by misuse of prescription drugs.[18]

Drug abuse also contributes to crimes beyond the obvious charges of drug possession or sales. In 2002, 25 percent of local inmates jailed for property offenses committed their crimes to raise money for drugs, versus 5 percent of violent criminals. In 2004, 30 percent of state prison inmates held for property crimes admitted drug-related motives, versus 10 percent of violent criminals.[19]

Prohibition's critics reply that two legal drugs—alcohol and nicotine—cause greater damage to American society than all illegal drugs combined and have government approval. Between 1982 and 2004 drunk drivers killed 462,116 victims in the United States. An average 708,000 persons are injured by American drunk drivers each year.[20] Drinking also contributes to 40 percent of America's fatal home fires, roughly 1,000 per year.[21] Cirrhosis of the liver claims more than 26,000 American lives per year, with 95 percent of those cases resulting from alcoholism. Deaths from accidental alcohol poisoning exceed 1,300 per year, while 50,000 binge drinkers survive hospital visits.[22]

Alcohol-related crimes eclipse those linked to drugs. By 1996, 36 percent of all American prison inmates admitted being drunk when they committed their crimes. Violent offenders were the worst, including 41 percent of those in local jails, 38 percent in state lockups, and 20 percent in federal prisons. Seventy-five percent of victims attacked by their spouses blamed alcohol. In an average year, 500,000 victims of alcohol-related violence report financial losses exceeding $400 million. In terms of property crimes, 22 percent of local offenders and 30 percent of state prison inmates are intoxicated during the offense.[23]

Tobacco, while rarely associated with crime, also inflicts a heavy toll. The U.S. Fire Administration blames 1,000 deaths per year on careless smokers who start fires at home. The CDC reports 438,000 deaths from tobacco-related disease each year, including 38,000 nonsmokers killed by inhaling secondhand smoke. The World Health Organization tabulates 5.4 million tobacco-related deaths per year, worldwide, and expects the number to reach 8.3 million by 2030.[24]

A final argument against drug prohibition involves unfair enforcement. Federal legislation reserves the harshest mandatory penalties for crack cocaine (normally used by low-income addicts), versus the powder cocaine preferred by more affluent (and mostly white) users. In 1995 the U.S. Sentencing Commission acknowledged racial injus-

FRANK LUCAS

Best known today from his portrayal by actor Denzel Washington in the 2007 film *American Gangster,* Frank Lucas is a native of North Carolina, born in 1930. He moved to New York City's Harlem ghetto as a young man, becoming a trusted aide to African-American gangster Ellsworth "Bumpy" Johnson (1905-68). At Johnson's death, Lucas assumed control of Harlem's rackets and challenged the Mafia for control of New York's heroin trade.

In pursuit of that goal, Lucas created a network of black military personnel to smuggle Asian heroin from Thailand and South Vietnam to New York. While some reports claim that drugs were smuggled in coffins containing the bodies of U.S. casualties from Vietnam, and Lucas admitted hiring a carpenter to build caskets with false bottoms for that purpose, accomplice Leslie Atkinson—portrayed as "Nate" by Roger Guenveur Smith in *American Gangster*—insists that the heroin was shipped in furniture, not coffins. In any case, the volume and purity of "Blue Magic" heroin imported by Lucas made him a multimillionaire, with office buildings in four states and a ranch in North Carolina, populated by 300 prime cattle and a $125,000 breeding bull.[25]

DEA agents and New York Police Department (NYPD) officers raided Lucas's New Jersey home in January 1975, seizing $584,683 in cash. Convictions in state and federal court earned him prison terms totaling 70 years, whereupon he turned state's evidence against his fellow traffickers, producing 100 more convictions. In 1981, after serving five years, Lucas was released into lifetime parole. Three years later police caught Lucas trying to exchange an ounce of heroin for a kilo of cocaine. Defended by the same lawyer who once prosecuted him, he received a seven-year sentence and was released in 1991.[26]

tice in drug sentencing, but Congress ignored the problem. A similar report, published in 2001 by the National Research Council called present sentencing guidelines "unconscionable," but the system remains unchanged.[27]

Commercial Crimes

Houston, Texas

Enron Corporation began life as Northern Natural Gas, a Nebraska company founded in 1932. In 1985 it bought Houston Natural Gas, changed its name to Enron, and moved its headquarters to Texas. CEO Kenneth Lay was one of America's highest-paid corporate leaders, earning $42.4 million in 1999. He was also a close friend of George W. Bush, steering Enron donations of $1.5 million to Bush and the Republican Party between 1994 and 2000. When Bush was elected president, some observers predicted that he would name Lay as Secretary of the Treasury, but Bush chose Alcoa chairman Paul O'Neill instead.[1]

By that time, Enron was headed for trouble. The rumbles began in June 2000, when company executives started selling large blocks of Enron stock, causing prices to plummet on Wall Street. Temporary CEO Jeffrey Skilling resigned in August 2001, one day before Enron vice president Sherron Watkins warned Lay of improper accounting practices. Investigators later learned that Lay himself sold $300 million worth of stock, while urging Enron employees to buy more. In October 2001 Enron announced a financial loss of $618 million. Two weeks later, company spokesmen admitted that Enron had exaggerated profits by $586 million since 1991, thus artificially inflating stock prices. Enron declared bankruptcy on December 2, 2001, and fired 21,000 employees the following day.[2]

BUYERS BEWARE

Throughout history, dishonest merchants have increased their profits by cutting corners on the quality of merchandise they sell. In most cases, those shoddy items are simply a nuisance: toys that break quickly, build-it-yourself kits with parts missing, "fat-burning" creams that do nothing, and so on. In other cases, though, the products may be deadly.

Thalidomide is a drug developed by German chemists in 1953, used to treat cancer and leprosy. It is also a sedative, prescribed to fight morning sickness in pregnant women until 1962. Unfortunately, most physicians did not know that thalidomide causes severe birth defects in rats, rabbits, and primates—including human beings. Between 1956 and 1962, thalidomide recipients in Africa and Asia gave birth to 10,000 deformed babies. Many suffered from *phocomelia,* a condition where the arms and legs are shortened or missing, sometimes with hands and feet attached directly to the torso. In the United States, where FDA approval was denied, 17 cases were

A chemist conducts a test to determine food safety in August 2007, months after an estimated 3,600 cats and dogs were killed by contaminated pet food made in China. *AP Photo/Andy Wong*

recorded from drugs dispensed without FDA approval from a supply distributed to doctors by the Richardson Merrell company with the understanding that the drug was still under investigation.[3] The thalidomide scandal produced new regulations for the testing of drugs used on humans.

A similar case involved Rofecoxib, an anti-inflammatory drug developed by Merck & Company to relieve pain caused by arthritis and other disorders. Unlike thalidomide, Rofecoxib won approval from the FDA in May 1999 and was sold under various brand names including Ceoxx and Vioxx. Physicians worldwide prescribed it to more than 80 million patients before realizing that long-term use increased the risk of heart attacks and strokes.[4]

Merck withdrew Rofecoxib from sale in September 2004, after earning $2.5 billion from sales in the preceding year alone, and while no criminal charges were filed, a blizzard of lawsuits followed. By March 2006, Merck faced 190 class action suits and 10,000 individual cases claiming wrongful death or injury from Rofecoxib. In August 2005, Texas jurors found Merck liable for the death of 59-year-old Robert Ernst and ordered the firm to pay his widow $253.4 million (although Texas law caps punitive damages at $26.1 million). Three months later, jurors in New Jersey reached the opposite conclusion, ruling that Merck had issued ample warnings to doctors before a local patient suffered a mild heart attack. Cases tried in 2006 produced mixed results: a New Jersey judge dismissed one lawsuit; Texas jurors slapped Merck with another $32 million penalty for the death of an elderly patient (reduced to $1 million on appeal); and another New Jersey court awarded $13.5 million to survivors of heart attack victim John McDarby.[5]

Many recalls of unsafe products from China preceded the Chinese milk scandal of 2008. In 2007 alone, the Mattel toy company recalled 19 million toys produced in China, due to manufacturers using toxic lead-based paint. Other

(continues)

(continued)

companies recalled thousands of dolls, doll houses, toy trains, and sunglasses for the same reason, while Hasbro recalled nearly 2 million defective Easy-Bake Ovens, responsible for burning children's fingers. In Europe, toothpaste was recalled because it contained chemicals used to make antifreeze. The most widely reported case involved recall of pet food contaminated with melamine, which killed an estimated 3,600 cats and dogs in March and April 2007. That scandal resulted in a ban on Chinese-made pet food in the United States, Canada, the European Union, Australia, and New Zealand. While Chinese officials downplayed the extent of the problem, they charged Zheng Xiaoyu, former head of the nation's food and drug administration, with taking $850,000 in bribes from various manufacturers between 1998 and 2005. Upon conviction, Zheng was shot by a firing squad on July 10, 2007. Zhang Shuhong, co-owner of the company that supplied Mattel with its lead-painted toys, reportedly committed suicide one month later, on August 11, 2007.[6]

The Justice Department announced a criminal investigation of Enron in January 2002. The SEC filed fraud charges and ordered Enron to pay an $80 million fine in March. Treasurer Ben Glisan Jr. pled guilty to fraud in September and received a five-year prison term. Three months later, an Enron subsidiary, Pacific Gas & Electric, agreed to an $8.5 million settlement for illegal trading practices in California and Oregon. Enron finance chief Andrew Fastow received a 10-year sentence in January 2004, while his wife was jailed for one year. Enron vice president Richard Causey pled guilty to securities fraud in December 2005, receiving a sentence of five to seven years. Jurors convicted Ken Lay on five counts and Jeffrey Skilling on 19, in May 2006, but Lay died prior to sentencing and his conviction was later vacated. Skilling received a prison term of 24 years and four months.[7]

The Enron scandal embarrassed President Bush and Vice President Dick Cheney, who held a series of meetings with Enron leaders and other corporate executives to chart America's energy policies in early 2001. The secret nature of those meetings violated federal law, and Cheney's refusal to produce transcripts over the next eight years fueled rumors of corruption and conspiracy.

WHEN COMPANIES ARE "PEOPLE"

We all recognize that corporations are made up of people—the owners, stockholders, and workers—but a company itself may also be a "legal person" under rulings issued by American and British courts. The concept dates from the U.S. Supreme Court case of *Santa Clara County v. Southern Pacific Railroad,* a suit over taxation, which declared in 1886 that "juristic persons"—groups of humans formed for a specific purpose, or corporations—may possess some of the rights enjoyed by flesh-and-blood citizens. Britain followed America's lead in the 1897 case of *Salomon v. Salomon,* a dispute centered around a London shoe company, and more than a century later, Australia's Corporation Act of 2001 declared corporations to be "legal persons."

A corporation's "human rights" are broad but not unlimited. It cannot vote, but it may own property, sign contracts, and file lawsuits (or be sued) in court. And corporations may be charged with crimes, punished with fines or other sanctions, though the company itself cannot be sent to prison. Many critics of the "legal person" concept feel such charges have been filed too seldom, and that punishments imposed on outlaw corporations are too lenient.

INSIDE JOBS

Bandits have been robbing banks at gunpoint since the 1860s—1,561 holdups across the United States in the last three months of 2007 alone—but the largest hauls result from "inside jobs" by trusted bank employees. Sometimes the looting is so flagrant that it topples banks and shatters public faith in government. [8]

Savings and loan (S&L) associations have existed in the United States since 1816, created as alternatives to banks, which catered mainly to the wealthiest Americans. Federal law limited the type and size of loans granted by S&Ls until October 16, 1982, when President Ronald Reagan signed the Garn-St. Germain Depository Institutions Act,

ADELPHIA COMMUNICATIONS CORPORATION

John Rigas founded Adelphia Communications at Couder-sport, Pennsylvania, in 1952 and took the company public in 1986. By the start of the 21st century, Adelphia had grown to become America's fifth-largest cable company, with 110,000 long-distance telephone customers in 27 states, but internal corruption forced the firm into bankruptcy in 2002.[9]

The company's main problem was theft by its owners, John Rigas and his son Timothy. While the full scope of their larceny may never be known, an audit conducted in 2002 revealed $2.3 billion in debts omitted from Adelphia's financial records. In July 2004, federal jurors convicted John and Timothy Rigas on 15 counts of bank fraud, securities fraud, and conspiracy. Another Rigas son, Michael, was acquitted of conspiracy, but jurors deadlocked on the other charges and failed to reach a verdict.[10] John Rigas received a 15-year prison term, while Timothy was sentenced to 20 years. Sixteen months later, Michael Rigas pled guilty to one count of falsifying company records. In March 2006 he was sentenced to 10 months' home confinement and two years' probation.[11]

While Adelphia's investors and creditors lost more than $150 million, the company's long-distance telephone customers were spared loss of service when Pioneer Telephone purchased Adelphia's network for $1.2 million in July 2005. Time Warner Cable and Comcast later purchased the majority of Adelphia's remaining assets.[12]

removing most restrictions on the industry. At the signing ceremony, Reagan said, "I think we've hit the jackpot."[13]

And the thieves agreed.

New S&Ls sprang up from coast to coast, often with shady characters in charge. Stock swindler Ivan Boesky bought an S&L in upstate New York; Neil Bush, son of then-Vice President George H.W. Bush, emerged as director of Denver's Silverado Savings and Loan; and corrupt lawyer Charles Keating took control of Lincoln Savings and Loan in Phoenix, Arizona. Unrestrained by Congress, S&Ls issued huge loans to unreliable borrowers and invested millions of dollars in high-yield "junk bonds" subject to wild fluctuations in value. When those investments failed, some S&L directors falsified their ledgers to conceal their losses. By 1986, Lincoln Savings alone had $135 million in unreported losses.[14]

Soon, the bankrupt S&Ls began to topple like a chain of dominoes. Between 1986 and 1989 the Federal Home Loan Bank Board closed 296 S&Ls with assets of $125 billion. The Resolution Trust Corporation, formed to deal with the crisis in 1989, closed 747 more with assets of $394 billion by 1995.[15] Millions of investors lost their savings overnight.

Normally, when bandits rob a bank, they are arrested, tried, and sent to prison. The S&L crisis was not a normal robbery, however. It was vast, almost beyond imagination, and the men involved had high-level political connections. Charles Keating donated $1.3 million to five U.S. Senators, and then asked them to help him avoid punishment. The "Keating Five," as they were called, soon faced investigation by the Senate for their efforts. Three—Alan Cranston, Dennis DeConcini, and Donald Riegel—were formally censured and lost their next re-election bids. Two others, John Glenn and John McCain, were cleared of ethics violations but criticized for "poor judgment."[16]

None of it helped Keating, whom California jurors convicted on 17 counts of fraud, racketeering, and conspiracy in December 1991. Four months later, he received a 10-year prison term. A federal court convicted Keating on 73 identical counts in January 1993, imposing a 12½-year sentence plus a $122 million fine. Keating's son-in-law pled guilty to fraud in May 1992 and received a 40-month sentence.

The other S&L bandits got lucky. The Federal Deposit Insurance Corporation sued Neil Bush and other Silverado executives, and Silverado settled out of court, with Bush paying $50,000 toward Silverado's losses of $1 billion. Even that was painless, since the Republican Party raised money to cover Neil's settlement. In February 1989, Neil's father—then President of the United States—approved a plan to support the failed S&L's with $160 billion in taxpayers' money.[17] A similar, but even more severe bank crisis struck America in 2008, prompting another congressional bailout. While Congress approved expenditure of $700 billion to rescue banks that suffered serious mismanagement, some observers predicted a final price tag of $4 *trillion*.[18]

Congress suffered its own banking scandal in 1992, when auditors revealed that 355 House members (out of 435 total) had written bad checks on their House Bank accounts. The 22 worst offenders had bounced 11,080 checks over three years, with five offenders accumulating bad debts exceeding $1.5 million. While check fraud is a crime, routinely leading to trial and prison, only one of the 355—House Sergeant at Arms Carl Perkins—faced trial on fraud charges, receiving a 21-month prison sentence. As a result of the House Bank investigation, 11 of the 22 worst offenders lost their bids for re-election, and four representatives pled guilty on criminal charges unrelated to the House Bank scandal.[19]

CHEATING UNCLE SAM

General Electric Corporation (GE) was founded by Thomas Edison in 1890, 14 years after he invented the electric light bulb. By mid-century, GE was America's ninth-largest industrial company, proud of its motto "We Bring Good Things to Life," but that pride has been tarnished by a long series of criminal cases including the following:

- In 1961 GE pled guilty to price-fixing and paid a $372,000 fine.
- In 1977 the company logged another price-fixing conviction.
- In 1979 GE settled a lawsuit filed by the state of Alabama over toxic chemicals dumped into rivers, and was fined $460 million by the Environmental Protection Agency.
- In 1981 GE was convicted of paying $1.25 million in bribes to Puerto Rican officials.
- In 1985 GE pled guilty to 108 counts of defrauding the U.S. Air Force on a contract to update Minuteman ballistic missiles. The company paid a $1 million fine and one of its chief engineers was convicted of perjury.
- In a separate 1985 case, GE pled guilty to falsifying employee time cards.

- In 1989 GE paid the government $3.5 million to settle litigation charging fraud at a jet-engine plant, where 9,000 labor vouchers were falsified to inflate billing.
- In 1990 GE was convicted of criminal fraud on a contract for U.S. Army battlefield computers, paying $16 million in fines.
- In 1992 GE again pled guilty to further defense contract frauds and paid a $69 million fine.
- In 1995 the Justice Department announced that GE would pay $7.1 million to settle yet another lawsuit claiming contract fraud.
- In 1997 GE paid $950,000 to settle charges that it faked test results on hundreds of circuit boards in aircraft engines, without conducting any tests.
- In 2004 the Securities and Exchange Commission (SEC) announced a settlement of charges that GE illegally concealed records of retirement benefits paid between 1997 and 2002.[20]

Incredibly, despite that record of criminal fraud spanning five decades, GE continues to receive lucrative government contracts, worth nearly $13 billion during 1997-2003. One watchdog agency, the Project on Government Oversight, suggests that GE's good fortune arises from huge political donations, approaching $6.2 billion during 1998-2004.[21] In June 2009, GE was poised to benefit from another government bailout, this one intended for banks. The company's original request totaled $140 billion.[22]

GE is not the only firm favored with federal contracts despite guilty pleas and convictions for defrauding the U.S. government. Others include Boeing, Grumman, Hughes, Lockheed, McDonnell Douglas, Northrop, Rockwell, and Teledyne—all recipients of multiple contracts that dwarf the amounts paid in civil and criminal fines.[23]

An unusually violent case of corporate crime emerged in March 2007, when the U.S. Department of Justice fined the Ohio-based Chiquita Brands fruit company $25 million for supporting terrorist groups in Colombia. In the 1950s, when it was known as United Fruit, the company collaborated with CIA agents to replace Guatemala's elected government with military rule, resulting in an estimated 140,000 to 250,000 deaths or disappearances.[24] On March 19, 2007, in federal court, Chiquita Brands admitted that it paid right-wing guerrillas at least $1.7 million to "protect" its Colombian workers between 1989 and

IMCLONE

ImClone Systems is a pharmaceutical company, created in 1984 to develop medicines for cancer treatment. In 2001 it developed a new drug called Erbitux, designed to slow

Dr. Samuel Waksal, former chief executive at ImClone Systems, is sworn in on Capitol Hill on June 13, 2002, prior to testifying before a House Commerce subcommittee regarding the accusation of securities fraud. Waksal pled guilty in June 2003, and received a seven-year prison sentence. *AP Photo/Dennis Cook*

2004. Those groups included the National Liberation Army, the Revolutionary Armed Forces of Colombia, and the United Self-Defense Forces of Colombia—all listed as terrorists by the U.S. State Department.[25]

Chiquita's settlement with Justice in America did not end the company's legal problems. In November 2007, relatives of Colombian murder victims sued Chiquita Brands for $7.86 billion, based on the company's financial support for terrorist groups linked to numerous slayings. One of the plaintiffs' attorneys, Terry Collingsworth, told reporters, "This is a landmark

the spread of colon cancer to other bodily organs. Unfortunately, the U.S. Food and Drug Administration (FDA) refused to approve sale of Erbitux that December, a decision that threatened ImClone with financial losses. Before the FDA's decision was announced, ImClone founder Samuel Waksal warned selected investors of the setback and advised them to sell off their stock before prices declined. Those who took the hint and sold in time included Waksal's father ($8.1 million), his daughter ($2.5 million), ImClome's vice president ($2.1 million), its general counsel ($2.5 million), and TV celebrity Martha Stewart ($200,000).[26]

Investigators for the SEC noted the rash of ImClone sales in late December 2001 and filed criminal charges of *insider trading*—the sale or purchase of stock based on corporate knowledge concealed from the general public. Samuel Waksal pled guilty to securities fraud in June 2003, receiving a sentence of seven years and three months in prison. Prosecutors also indicted Martha Stewart, and while she denied any wrongdoing, jurors convicted her on three counts in July 2004. Stewart received a sentence of five months in jail, five months of home confinement, and two years probation.

New clinical tests on Erbitux secured FDA approval for its sale in 2004, but it came too late to save ImClone. The company went up for sale in 2006 but failed to find a buyer. In April 2007 the *Wall Street Journal* reported ImClone's announcement that Erbitux failed to prolong the lives of pancreatic cancer victims.

---

case, maybe the biggest terrorism case in history. In terms of casualties, it's the size of three World Trade Center attacks."[27] Days later, on December 7, 2007, prosecutors in Medellín called on Chiquita's nine board members to answer charges that their company "for years made payments to paramilitary structures and participated in the logistics to enter arms that these groups used to massacre, torture, disappear, and forcibly displace thousands of peasants" in the Colombian district of Urabá Antioquia.[28] Those cases remained unsettled as this book went to press.

6

Corrupting Authority

New York City

On April 6, 2006, federal jurors convicted two Mafia gunmen on charges of racketeering, extortion, obstructing justice, and eight counts of first-degree murder. Most of the victims were gangsters themselves, but one—Nicholas Guido—had been killed by mistake, in a case of mistaken identity. The defendants, Louis Eppolito and Stephen "The Stick" Caracappa, were also convicted of plotting to kill an informant whose testimony sent Mafia boss John Gotti to prison for life. The hitmen, too, received life terms on June 5, 2006.

New Yorkers are accustomed to such trials, but this one was unique.

The killers were detectives with the New York Police Department (NYPD), assigned to investigate organized crime.

FBI agents identified Eppolito and Caracappa as crooked cops in 1985 but took no action at the time. Eppolito tried to spin the evidence in 1992, when he published a book titled *Mafia Cop: The Story of an Honest Cop Whose Family Was the Mob.* Two years later, mob informant Anthony Casso revealed that Eppolito and Caracappa had received $375,000 in bribes and contract murder payments since 1985. Even then, it took 11 more years for prosecutors to indict the detectives, with various mobsters, in March 2005.[1] Both defendants claimed discrimination, on the basis of their Italian-American heritage, but an appellate court upheld their convictions in September 2008.

Mafia hitman and former New York City police officer Louis Eppolito (left) exits Brooklyn Federal Court escorted by his lawyer in July 2005. Eppolito received a life sentence after being found guilty of eight counts of first-degree murder, among other crimes. *AP Photo/Louis Lanzano*

Criminal groups like the Mafia operate best when police and prosecutors fail to do their jobs. Sometimes that corruption reaches to the highest levels.

Former New York City policeman Stephen Caracappa leaves
Brooklyn Federal Court in July 2005. In April 2006, Caracappa
and fellow former NYPD officer Louis Eppolito were convicted on
charges of racketeering, extortion, obstruction of justice, and eight
counts of first-degree murder. *AP Photo/Louis Lanzano*

"I AM NOT A CROOK"

Those words, spoken by President Richard Nixon in November 1973,
came back to haunt him nine months later, when he resigned in disgrace

to avoid impeachment by Congress. Today, it's known that gangsters, shady businessmen, and corrupt labor unions were among those who bankrolled Nixon's political career from the start in 1946. That same link to corruption ultimately brought him down.

Nixon served in the House of Representatives from 1947 to 1950, in the Senate from 1950 to 1953, and as vice president from 1953 to 1960. He lost the 1960 presidential race, thanks in part to organized crime's support for opponent John F. Kennedy, but won in 1968 with a promise of strict "law and order," including a federal war against organized crime. Once in office, however, Nixon released notorious mobsters from prison, sold ambassadorships to the highest bidders, and continued accepting illegal donations. By 1972, seeking re-election in the midst of protests against the Vietnam War, Nixon was obsessed with crushing individuals and groups he viewed as personal enemies.[2]

To that end, Nixon's campaign manager, former Attorney General John Mitchell, approved a series of "dirty tricks" against those who criticized Nixon. Tactics ranged from petty harassment to burglary and tax audits by the Internal Revenue Service. On June 17, 1972, five agents of Mitchell's Committee to Re-Elect the President (CREEP) were caught burglarizing Democratic Party headquarters at the Watergate office complex in Washington, D.C. Subsequent investigations, including a series of public hearings before the U.S. Senate, revealed that the Watergate break-in was merely the tip of the iceberg.

Nixon conspired with aides to conceal the crimes committed on his behalf, but that campaign failed when one assistant, John Dean III, announced that Nixon had recorded private conversations at the White House. Nixon reluctantly obeyed court orders to surrender the tapes—including sessions where he joined in discussions of bribery and other crimes—and his fate was sealed. Nixon announced his resignation on August 8, 1974, and left Washington the next day. On September 8, President Gerald Ford pardoned Nixon for any crimes he may have committed as president.

While Nixon escaped punishment, his aides were less fortunate. All five Watergate burglars were convicted and sent to prison, along with break-in planners Howard Hunt and Gordon Liddy. John Dean avoided prison by testifying against his ex-colleagues, but he was disbarred from

THE KNAPP COMMISSION

Frank Serpico joined the NYPD in 1959 and served 12 years as a patrolman before his promotion to the Vice Squad. There, he encountered widespread corruption but refused to accept the bribes shared by his fellow officers. That attitude soon left him virtually friendless, enduring harassment from those who collected the underworld payoffs. Serpico reported the pervasive corruption to his superiors in 1967, but they did nothing until the *New York Times* broke the story in April 1970. Mayor John Lindsay then created a special commission, led by attorney Whitman Knapp (1909-2004), to investigate the charges made by Serpico and another honest cop, Sergeant David Durk.

The Knapp investigation spanned two years, including a series of public hearings launched in October 1971, but Serpico nearly missed the proceedings. On the night of February 3, 1971, during a Brooklyn drug raid, he was shot in the face by a narcotics dealer. Three other officers were present, but they failed to report the shooting, leaving a civilian bystander to make the call. Serpico survived, now deaf in his left ear, and testified before the Knapp Commission after he recovered.

The commission's final report, published in December 1972, revealed extensive corruption within the NYPD, where officers were known as "grass eaters" (those taking minor bribes under peer pressure) or "meat eaters" (those who aggressively pursued large payoffs). Various reforms were recommended, including creation of an Internal Affairs

practicing law. Jurors convicted John Mitchell, with White House aides John Ehrlichman and H.R. Haldeman, in February 1975, sending all three to prison for 18 months. CREEP conspirators Charles Colson, Egil Krogh Jr., and Jeb Magruder pled guilty to various charges and served prison time. So did one of Nixon's secretaries, Dwight Chapin, charged with perjury. In California, Lieutenant Governor Edwin Reinecke was convicted of lying to a Watergate grand jury. He resigned in October 1974, then ran for governor a month later and lost.

New York City detective Frank Serpico, with beard, sits in front of his attorney at the Knapp Commission's investigation of police corruption in New York on December 13, 1971. *AP Photo/Jim Wells*

Division to investigate police misconduct of all kinds. Opinions differ as to whether the reforms had the desired effect. Corruption scandals like the case of Stephen Caracappa and Louis Eppolito still embarrass the department.

Frank Serpico was promoted to detective in May 1971, but retired from the NYPD in June 1972 and spent the next 10 years in Europe. Two weeks after Serpico retired, Whitman Knapp became a federal judge and held that post until his death in June 2004.

Despite the scandal that ended his political career, Richard Nixon suffered no lasting hardship. He lived in luxury and traveled widely, earned millions from sale of his memoirs in 1990, and was eulogized as a great statesman at his funeral, in April 1994. Meanwhile, dozens of public scandals in the past three decades have been christened with the suffix "-gate," in memory of Watergate. They range from serious events such as "Filegate" (illegal examination of FBI files by members of the Clinton administration in 1993-94) to bizarre cases like "Camillagate" (tape recordings of phone conversations between Britain's Prince Charles and mistress Camilla Parker Bowles in 1993) and "Fajitagate" (a brawl over Mexican food, involving San Francisco policemen in 2002).

COPS AND ROBBERS

Police are only human, and some go bad despite their oath to uphold and enforce the law. Around the world, throughout the history of law enforcement, officers have disgraced themselves by accepting bribes, collaborating with criminals, and faking evidence to "frame" innocent persons. Few police departments have escaped some measure of embarrassment by "bad apples" on the payroll. And when cops turn to robbers, no one is safe.

One of America's earliest cases involved NYPD Lieutenant Charles Becker, a brutal officer who extorted cash from Manhattan brothels and gamblers between 1893 and 1912. In July 1912, he ordered the murder of gambler Herman Rosenthal, who had complained to the press about Becker's corruption. Convicted at trial, Becker was executed in New York's electric chair on July 30, 1915.

Thirty years after Chicago's police chief complained that half of his men were involved in illegal bootlegging, little had changed in the Windy City. Liquor was legal, but many police still took bribes from gangsters, and some went even further. In 1960, eight officers from the Summerdale district on Chicago's Northwest Side were convicted of moonlighting as burglars. The resultant scandal forced Mayor Richard Daley to appoint a new police commissioner.

Miami, Florida, has been the scene of frontline action in America's drug wars since the 1970s, and sometimes it is difficult to tell the cops and gangsters apart. In 1985 a group of renegade officers robbed drug dealers along the Miami River, selling the stolen cocaine themselves. In one July raid, three smugglers leaped from their boat and drowned in the river, prompting an investigation that sent 18 present and former policemen to prison on various charges, including murder.

In early 1993, New York state trooper David Harding applied for a job with the Central Intelligence Agency (CIA). When asked if he was willing to break the law, Harding described several cases in which he and other members of the New York State Police fabricated evidence to convict persons they believed to be guilty of crimes. Instead of hiring him, the CIA reported Harding's confession to state authorities, resulting in felony convictions of Harding and four other officers. Their prison terms ranged from 2½ to 12 years.

The Los Angeles Police Department (LAPD) has been rocked by periodic scandals since the 1920s, but one of the worst emerged in the late 1990s, with exposure of lawless behavior by officers assigned to the Rampart Division's anti-gang unit. More than 70 officers were implicated in crimes that included torture, theft, drug-dealing, bank robbery, perjury, planting evidence, and framing innocent persons. A police administrative board found sufficient evidence to fire five officers, while seven more resigned and 12 were suspended for various periods. The case spawned 160 lawsuits, costing the city $125 million in settlements, and resulted in 106 convictions being overturned on grounds of tainted evidence. A wrongful-death lawsuit in 2007 blamed two Rampart officers for the 1997 murder of rap star Christopher Wallace, better known as "The Notorious B.I.G."[3]

Even the FBI is not immune to corruption. In the late 1950s, Agent Harold Rico forged an unholy alliance with Boston gangster James Bulger, using Bulger to obtain information about the New England Mafia. In 1965 Rico suppressed evidence that Bulger's gang had murdered victim Edward Deegan, remaining silent while prosecutors convicted four innocent men of that crime. Defendants Louis Greco and Henry Tamelo died in prison, while Peter Limone and Joe Salvati remained in custody until 1997 and 2001, respectively. When his role in the frame-up was revealed, Rico sneered at reporters, saying, "What do you want, tears?"[4]

Rico's wrongdoing was not limited to suppression of evidence. In October 2003 he was indicted for the May 1981 Oklahoma murder of millionaire victim Roger Wheeler. Rico died in jail three months later, before facing trial, but former Boston agent John Connolly Jr. was not so fortunate. In 2007 he received a 10-year prison term for bribery, racketeering, and other offenses (he warned James Bulger of an impending federal indictment, which allowed Bulger to flee the country). A year later, Connolly was convicted of murder and conspiracy in the 1982 Florida slaying of John Callahan, a witness against Bulger's gang who was slain by the same hitman who shot Roger Wheeler. Jurors convicted Connolly of second-degree murder on November 6, 2008.

GOVERNMENTS FOR SALE

Gangsters are not alone in bribing government officials. Many corporations "grease the wheels" of government with cash and other favors in America and all around the world, obtaining tax-exemptions, fat contracts, and other benefits denied to firms that practice honest commerce. In that respect, few companies can rival Lockheed Corporation, an American aerospace firm founded in 1912, which changed its name to Lockheed Martin in 1995.

Lockheed's corruption first surfaced in 1957, when company agents bribed officials of the Japanese Air Self-Defense Force to buy the company's F-104 jet fighters instead of Grumman's F-11 Super Tigers. Five years later, according to Lockheed lobbyist Ernest Hauser, the company paid Germany's Minister of Defense $10 million to approve purchase of 900 F-104s. Documents related to that deal were shredded in 1962, but the scandal persisted through German election campaigns in 1976. That same year, in U.S. Senate hearings, Lockheed's vice chairman admitted paying Japanese Prime Minister Kakuei Tanaka $3 million to select Lockheed's L-1011 aircraft over the DC-10 made by McDonnell Douglas. Tanaka was arrested in July 1976 and received a four-year prison term in 1983, but died without serving time. Overall, Senate investigators reported, Lockheed had paid $22 million to various foreign officials, but the amount may well have been greater. *Time* magazine claimed that Lockheed used Saudi arms dealer Adnan Khashoggi as a middleman for payoffs, giving him $106 million in "commissions" between 1970 and 1975.[5]

The 1976 revelations did not change Lockheed's practices. A statement from Prince Bernhard of Holland, published after his death in 2004, confessed that he accepted $1.1 million from Lockheed in the 1970s, to ensure government purchase of F-104 fighters. Italy's president, prime minister, and two cabinet ministers were also paid for their agreement to buy Lockheed's C-130 Hercules transport planes for the Italian Air Force. One crashed in March 1977, killing the crew and 38 cadets on board. Those crimes prompted Congress to pass the Corrupt

Foreign Practices Act in 1977, and forced Italian President Giovanni Leone's resignation in June 1978, but little changed at Lockheed.

In June 1994, a federal grand jury indicted Lockheed and two former executives for paying an Egyptian lawmaker, Leila Takla, $1.8 million to arrange the government's $79 million purchase of three transport planes. Allen Love, former director of Lockheed's Middle East and North African sales division, pled guilty in January 1995, while Lockheed was convicted and fined $24.8 million. Five years later, the company paid another $4.25 million in fines for misusing funds received on a contract to upgrade the Egyptian navy's sonar system. In June 2004, Lockheed's plan to purchase Titan Corporation in San Diego fell through after Titan was accused of bribing officials in Benin and Saudi Arabia.[6]

COUNTRIES FOR SALE

Kleptocracy is the term used for governments run by self-serving criminals, often dictators or small, ruling families, who loot nations for their personal benefit. In the process, human rights are frequently trampled and disease and poverty flourish for all but the wealthy people in charge, while government service declines and aggressive military actions claim thousands of lives.

Such governments are hardly new. Roman emperors Caligula (A.D. 37-41) and Nero (A.D. 54-68) were notorious for their greed and corruption, meeting their respective ends by assassination and suicide. In America, political bosses such as New York's William Tweed, Jersey City's Frank Hague, Chicago's William Thompson, Boston's James Curley, Ohio's Mark Hannah, and Missouri's Tom Pendergast ranked among the most infamous. Still, at their worst, the Americans could not compare to certain kleptocrats listed by the international watchdog group Transparency International in 2004. The dubious prize-winners included:

○ Indonesian President Suharto (1921-2008), who stole at least $15 billion, perhaps $35 billion, between 1967 and his forced resignation in 1998.
○ Ferdinand Marcos (1917-89), who ruled the Philippines from 1965 to 1986, crushing political dissent and stealing between $5 billion and $10 billion.

- President Mobutu Sese Seko of Zaire (1930-97), who looted his country of $5 billion before revolution and terminal illness drove him into exile.
- General Sani Abacha (1943-98), who seized control of Nigeria by force in 1993 and stole an estimated $1 billion per year until a heart attack claimed his life.
- Slobodan Milošević (1941-2006), one-time president of Yugoslavia, who relieved taxpayers of $1 billion between 1997 and 2000. His brutal campaigns of "ethnic cleansing" prompted Milošević's trial for war crimes, but he died in jail before a verdict was delivered.
- Dr. François "Papa Doc" Duvalier (1907-71), who used violence and voodoo to terrorize Haiti from 1957 until his death, killing thousands and banking untold millions in the process. Son Jean-Claude "Baby Doc" Duvalier upheld the family tradition from 1971 to 1986, when he fled the island with an estimated $300 million to $800 million.
- Peruvian President Alberto Fujimori, born to Japanese immigrant parents in 1938, who held office from 1990 to 2000. Corruption and repression sparked rebellion in Peru, and Fujimori fled to Japan with an estimated $600 million, then traveled to Chile, where he was arrested in 2005. In 2007 he received a six-year prison sentence for abuse of presidential powers, and was fined 400,000 soles ($135,000).
- Pavlo Lazarenko, the most energetic thief on the list, who stole an estimated $200 million dollars during his 13 months as Ukrainian prime minister in 1996-97. He subsequently fled to Switzerland, but was arrested there in 1998, then posted $3 million bail and made his way to the United States. American prosecutors refused extradition to Ukraine but tried Lazarenko in federal court for fraud and money-laundering. He received a nine-year prison term in August 2006.
- José Arnoldo Alemán Lacayo, president of Nicaragua from 1997 to 2002, who used his office to accumulate a personal fortune of $100 million. He was indicted on corruption charges in December 2002 and received a 20-year sentence in December 2003.

TEAPOT DOME

The election of President Warren Harding in 1920 brought his "Ohio Gang" to Washington and launched an era of corruption unrivaled until Richard Nixon took office in 1969. Bribes were so common under Attorney General Harry Daugherty that reporters nicknamed the Department of Justice the "Department of Easy Virtue,"[7] but the worst thief was Secretary of the Interior Albert Fall. Fall's department controlled America's oil reserves, intended for emergency use by the U.S. Navy, but in 1921 Fall decided the reserves were unneeded. Harry Sinclair, owner of Mammoth Oil, "loaned" Fall $100,000 in return for access to the government oilfields at Teapot Dome, Montana, while Edward Doheny of American Petroleum "loaned" another $385,000 for rights to drill in oilfields at Elk Hills, California.

The *Wall Street Journal* exposed Fall's activities in April 1922, prompting a Senate investigation of what became known as the Teapot Dome Scandal. Despite obstruction by Attorney General Daugherty and FBI Director William Burns, the facts were slowly brought to light. Fall resigned in March 1923, and President Harding died five months later, before the full scope of Fall's crimes was exposed. Jurors convicted Fall of bribery in 1929, whereupon he was fined $100,000 and received a one-year prison term. Harry Sinclair served a short jail term for jury-tampering and paid a $100,000 fine for contempt of Congress. Edward Doheny faced charges of attempted bribery, but he was acquitted in 1930.

o Joseph Ejercito Estrada, an actor who was elected president of the Philippines in June 1998 and ruled until January 2001, when he was impeached. His trial on charges of stealing an estimated $80 million lasted from April 2001 to September 2007, when he was convicted. A month later, President Maria Gloria Macapagal-Arroyo granted Ejercito a full pardon.[8]

Dictators, as a rule, are generally corrupt. The worst in modern history was Adolf Hitler, whose Nazi minions plundered banks, art galleries, and private homes throughout Europe and western Russia between 1933 and 1945. In 1940, Hitler named colleague Alfred Rosenberg as Reich Minister for the Occupied Eastern Territories (Russia, Ukraine, and the Baltic states), where his agents stole 21,903 pieces of art. The total for Europe at large surpassed 100,000 identified artworks, many of which remain missing today. Billions of dollars in cash, gems, and precious metals (including gold from the teeth of victims murdered in death camps) were banked in neutral Switzerland or shipped abroad to finance Nazi movements in Latin America. The rightful owners of those treasures who survived the Holocaust are still struggling to recover their lost property, more than 60 years after Hitler's suicide in Berlin.[9]

Crimes Against Humanity

Republic of Srpska, Bosnia, and Herzegovina

On August 5, 2008, spokesmen for the Municipal Association for the Search for Prisoners-of-War and Missing Civilians from Brod announced discovery of five mass graves dating from 1992, when the former nation of Yugoslavia dissolved into chaotic civil war between hostile Serbs and Croats. That brutal conflict soon degenerated into "ethnic cleansing" fueled by racism and religious bigotry, spawning atrocities that included slaughter of whole towns and the establishment of concentration camps where Muslim women were caged and raped repeatedly by Serbian police and soldiers. Ten years later, Sarajevo's Research and Documentation Center calculated the final toll at 97,207 dead—57,523 soldiers and 39,684 civilians—while some 1.8 million were left homeless. Two-thirds of the dead were Muslims.[1]

The new discoveries around Brod included remains of 368 victims, with 23 murdered children among them. All of the 263 identified corpses were Serbs evacuated from Brod and four other nearby towns. Marko Grabovac, supervisor of the recovery effort, noted that 1,600 victims from the area were still missing. "At least half," he said, "were killed, their bodies thrown into the Sava river."[2]

INHUMAN ACTS

All crimes are committed by humans against other humans, but some transcend mere personal attacks, or even the acts of deranged individu-

Forensic experts inspect body remains at a mass-grave site outside of Sarajevo, Bosnia, in May 2008. Some 30,000 people went missing in Bosnia during the 1992–1995 war, and over the years experts have been finding their bodies in mass graves throughout the country. *AP Photo/Emel Emric*

als like Virginia Tech gunman Seung-Hui Cho. Such crimes, including large-scale atrocities targeting selected groups of people based on race, religion, nationality, or similar factors, are defined by international law as "crimes against humanity."

That term was first used in May 1915, when spokesmen for the Allied Powers in World War I accused Turkish leaders of slaughtering ethnic minorities in occupied territories. Thirty years later, referring to crimes committed by Nazi forces during World War II, the Nuremberg Charter listed specific crimes against humanity including "murder, extermination, enslavement, deportation, and other inhumane acts committed against any civilian population, before or during the war, or persecutions on political, racial or religious grounds... whether or not in violation of the domestic law of the country where perpetrated."[3]

In 2002 the United Nations established the International Criminal Court, whose Rome Statute lists specific acts as crimes against humanity when committed as part of a widespread attack against any civilian population, committed with official knowledge. Aside from the crimes identified in 1945, the list includes imprisonment, torture, various sexual assaults (including forced pregnancy, prostitution, or sterilization), enforced disappearance, and apartheid (the system of racial segregation practiced by South Africa from 1948 to 1993).[4]

REIGN OF TERROR

Many definitions are advanced for *terrorism*, but all include the elements of actual or threatened violence, carried out for psychological effect, often (but not always) targeting non-combatant civilians. Within that broad definition, three types of terrorism are recognized. *Repressive* terrorism is used by those in power to maintain control and suppress dissent. *Revolutionary* terrorism seeks to overthrow a government or some established institution. *Sub-revolutionary* terrorism is employed to alter a specific policy or "punish" perceived enemies.[5] History offers many examples of each.

Classic practitioners of repressive terror include Joseph Stalin (1878-1953), whose Great Purge of the 1930s officially killed 681,692 of his fellow Russians, with some estimates approaching 2 million;[6] China's Mao Zedong (1893-1976), blamed by some historians for a death toll in the tens of millions between 1949 and 1976;[7] Idi Amin (1925-2003), dictator of Uganda from 1971 to 1979, blamed for killing at least 100,000 victims, and perhaps as many as 500,000;[8] and Augusto Pinochet (1915-2006), whose military junta in Chile killed at least 2,279 victims during 1973-74, while torturing 30,000 others.[9]

Revolutionary terrorist groups have battled governments on every inhabited continent. A prime example, the Irish Republican Army, opposed British rule in Ireland from 1916 to 1923, when the Irish Republic was established. Even then, Britain retained control of six counties comprising Northern Ireland, and factions of the IRA continued their armed struggle until 2005, when a cease-fire was finally negotiated. More recently, the Muslim group al-Qaeda ("The Base," in Arabic) has attacked targets from the Middle East and Africa to Indonesia, Europe and the United States, pursuing relentless warfare against Israel and its allies. Al-Qaeda's most notorious crimes include bombings of American embassies in Kenya and Tanzania, which killed 223 victims and wounded more than 4,000 in August 1998, and the skyjackings that claimed 3,000 lives in the United States on September 11, 2001. Some sources also blame al-Qaeda for the London subway bombings of July 2005, which killed 56 persons and wounded 700.

Sub-revolutionary terrorists in the United States include the self-styled Army of God, composed of "pro-life" Christian extremists who oppose the Supreme Court's 1973 abortion ruling in *Roe v. Wade* by bombing and burning women's clinics, kidnapping and murdering clinic physicians or nurses, and harassing abortion providers with hoax mailings of "anthrax" powder. A group with different objectives, the Earth Liberation Front, practices "monkey-wrenching"—sabotage against corporations which, in the ELF's view, threaten Earth's environment. While no fatalities have yet resulted from ELF's actions, its spokesmen claim credit for arson attacks on buildings and construction equipment.

Some terrorist groups evolve and adopt new perspectives. The Ku Klux Klan has always been a violent racist group, but its goals have changed over the past 140-odd years. During Reconstruction (1866-76), the KKK practiced revolutionary terrorism against Republican "carpetbag" governments in the South, seeking restoration of white-supremacist Democratic rule. From its 1915 revival until 1944, the Klan joined racist police and politicians to practice repressive terrorism against minorities, labor unions, and "radicals." From 1945 through the 1960s, Klansmen waged sub-revolutionary terrorist campaigns against expanding civil rights for African Americans. Since the 1970s, some Klan groups have reverted to revolutionary violence, attacking the federal government, which they believe is controlled by traitors.

GENOCIDE

The worst crimes against humanity involve deliberate attempts to wipe out whole races, religions, or other large groups of people, defined as *genocide*. Lithuanian author Raphael Lemkin coined the term during World War II, while observing Nazi persecution of his fellow Jews in Eastern Europe.[10]

In 1948 the United Nations legally defined genocide as "any of the following acts committed with intent to destroy, in whole or in part, a national, ethnical, racial or religious group, as such: killing members of the group; causing serious bodily or mental harm to members of the group; deliberately inflicting on the group conditions of life, calculated to bring about its physical destruction in whole or in part; imposing measures intended to prevent births within the group; [and] forcibly transferring children of the group to another group."[11]

While genocide had no formal name before the 1940s, the concept is ancient. Many scholars regard American Indians as victims of genocide inflicted by European invaders between 1492 and 1890, when untold millions died by violence or from disease, starvation, enslavement, and deportation from their native lands. In parts of South America, deliberate slaughter of Indian tribes continued well into the 20th century. White Australians waged a similar campaign against aboriginal tribes for more than a century, beginning with the Bathurst massacre in 1824 and ending—at least, officially—with the Coniston massacre of 1928.

Stories of genocide emerge from every corner of the planet. Between 1904 and 1907, German troops under General Lothar von Trotha slaughtered 80 percent of the Herero tribe and half of their Nama neighbors—75,000 victims—in the region of present-day Namibia. Between 1914 and 1923, Turkish forces massacred an estimated 1.5 million Armenians; 360,000 Greeks; and 275,000 Assyrians. During 1919-20, Bolshevik troops killed or deported an estimated 300,000 to 500,000 Don Cossacks. Government confiscation of wheat from Ukraine and Kazakhstan in 1933 produced 6 million deaths from starvation.[12]

History's most famous case of genocide is the Holocaust of 1933-45, when Adolf Hitler's crusade to rid Europe of "inferior" peoples destroyed an estimated 5.9 million Jews, 2 to 3 million Soviet prisoners of war, 1.8 to 2 million Poles, 220,000 to 500,000 Gypsies, 200,000 to 250,000 disabled persons, 80,000 to 200,000 Freemasons, 5,000 to 15,000 gays, and 2,000 to 5,000 Jehovah's Witnesses. Those figures represent only deliberate murders, and do not include the 12 million military deaths recorded in Europe and North Africa during World War II.[13]

Sadly, the legal ban imposed in 1948 did not halt genocide. Such crimes continue to the present day, with examples including some 200,000 noncombatants murdered during Guatemala's civil war of 1960-96, an estimated 1.5 to 3 million victims killed when Bangladesh

ADOLF EICHMANN (1906–62)

Born in Germany and raised in Austria, Adolf Eichmann dropped out of high school to work as a mechanic, then a salesman. In April 1932 he joined the Austrian branch of Adolf Hitler's Nazi Party, advancing to the "elite" SS seven months later. He moved back to Germany in July 1933, after Nazis gained control of the government, and in November he became an administrator at Dachau's concentration camp for political prisoners. Advancing steadily through Nazi ranks, Eichmann served in Berlin, Palestine, and Austria during 1934-38. In 1939, after the start of World War II, he was assigned to lead a branch of the Reich Central Security Office devoted to expulsion of Jews from Germany. In 1941, when Hitler ordered mass-murder of Jews throughout Europe, Eichmann was named Transportation Administrator for the "Final Solution." From that post, he supervised shipment of millions to death camps in Poland.

At war's end in 1945, Eichmann was captured by U.S. soldiers but gave a false name and escaped the following year. He hid in Germany until 1950, and then fled to Argentina, where President Juan Perón welcomed fugitive war criminals. By then, the state of Israel had been formed, and its agents actively pursued Nazis around the world. An informant found

sought independence from Pakistan in 1971, the massacre of 200,000 persons during Indonesia's occupation of East Timor in 1975-99, another 500,000 slain during Ethiopia's "Red Terror" of 1977-78, some 937,000 Tutsi tribesmen killed by rival Hutus in Rwanda during 1994, and massacres of Pygmies during the Second Congo War, ongoing since 1998.[15]

WAR CRIMES

While most definitions of crimes against humanity focus on violence directed toward civilian noncombatants, soldiers may also be convicted of *war crimes* for various acts committed against rival military forces.

Eichmann in 1954, living in Buenos Aires as "Ricardo Klement." After long surveillance, agents snatched Eichmann from a street near his home on May 11, 1960, and flew him to Israel 10 days later.

Despite international protests against the kidnapping—a tactic later adopted by the United States as "extraordinary rendition" and used primarily during the War on Terror—Eichmann faced trial in Jerusalem on April 11, 1961. Seated inside a box of bulletproof glass, he heard witnesses describe his key role in the Holocaust, while ex-Nazis claimed he was merely a clerk, required to follow orders from his superiors. Testimony ended on August 14, and three judges convicted Eichmann on December 11. He received a death sentence, and Israel's Supreme Court denied his appeal on May 29, 1962. Two days later, he mounted the gallows at Ramla prison. Before the noose was placed around his neck, Eichmann said, "Long live Germany. Long live Austria. Long live Argentina. These are the countries with which I have been most closely associated and I shall not forget them. I had to obey the rules of war and my flag. I am ready."[15]

After his hanging, Eichmann's corpse was cremated and his ashes were scattered over the Mediterranean Sea, to deprive him of a final resting place and ensure that other Nazis could not build a monument at his grave site.

As defined by the International Criminal Court in 2002, those illegal acts include torture, denying fair trials to prisoners of war, forcing prisoners to serve in a hostile army, hostage-taking, killing soldiers who surrender, using poisoned weapons or human shields, drafting child soldiers, misusing flags of truce, and looting.[16]

Two notorious cases of war crimes involve the Malmedy massacre of 1944 and the My Lai massacre of 1968. In the first case, German troops executed 90 American soldiers captured in Belgium, during the Battle of the Bulge. Seventy defendants faced trial, of whom 43 were sentenced to death (though none were executed), 22 received life prison terms, and eight others got shorter sentences. The My Lai

POL POT (1925–98)

The Cambodian leader known as Pol Pot was born Saloth Sar, son of an affluent family descended from ancient Chinese-Khmer tribesmen. He studied in Paris during 1949–53, and joined the French Communist Party. Failing college grades cost him his scholarship in 1954, and he returned to Cambodia, promoting rebellion in imitation of Ho Chi Minh's guerrilla forces in neighboring Vietnam. Ten years elapsed before Pol Pot emerged as leader of the Khmer Rouge ("Red Khmer") insurgents, and the uprising he hoped for did not begin in earnest until January 1968. Even then, Khmer Rouge forces did not unseat Cambodia's military government until September 1975. Pol Pot then changed the country's name to Democratic Kampuchea and established his own dictatorship, persecuting a long list of victims that included Buddhists and Muslims; the physically disabled; ethnic Chinese, Laotians, and Vietnamese; Cambodians with any link to Western nations; and anyone with higher education.

By 1976 the Khmer Rouge government recognized three kinds of people: "base" citizens with full rights, "candidates" for full citizenship, and "depositees" evacuated from cities into rural communes, where they existed on two bowls of rice soup per day. Believing that only 1 or 2 million people were needed to build a communist paradise, Pol Pot set out to kill the other 6 to 7 million through forced labor, beatings, starvation, and live burial in mass graves. While no precise statistics are available, various sources claim that he supervised the death of at least 750,000 victims, perhaps as many as 2 million. Yale University's Cambodian Genocide Project places the figure at 1.7 million.[17]

massacre occurred in Vietnam, when American troops murdered at least 347 unarmed villagers (some reports claim 504). Twenty-six soldiers were charged with various crimes in that case, but only one—

Former Khmer Rouge leader Pol Pot, responsible for the death of millions of Cambodians, answers questions during a January 1998 interview. *AP Photo/ Prasit Saengrungruang/Bankgok Post*

A two-year war with Vietnam, beginning in 1977, weakened Pol Pot's control of the nation. He fled to Thailand in January 1979, posing as Cambodia's ruler in exile until 1986, when he moved on to China for cancer treatments. Khmer Rouge forces recaptured part of Cambodia in 1989, and Pol Pot returned to continue his fight for control. Partially paralyzed by a stroke in 1995, he battled on until November 1997, when dissident Khmer Rouge officers arrested him for the June massacre of a rival politician's family. On April 15, 1998, his former cohorts announced for Pol Pot's delivery to an international court, but he died that same night. Various sources blame his death on heart failure, suicide, or murder.

Lieutenant William Calley—was convicted. He received a two-year prison term and served less than five months under house arrest, by order of President Richard Nixon.[18]

8

Cybercrimes

Stansted Airport, Essex, England

Stansted is Britain's third-busiest airport, located 38 miles northeast of central London. It serves more than 40 airlines, moving people and cargo to and from Europe, America, Israel, India, and Malaysia. In any given year, more than 200,000 flights and 20 million passengers use its facilities.

For all that bustle, one event on March 3, 1995, was still unique. That afternoon, agents from Interpol and Scotland Yard were waiting in the transit lounge to greet a flight arriving from Moscow. The passenger they came to meet was not expecting them, nor was he pleased to see them. He left the terminal in handcuffs, headed for a prison cell.

Vladimir Levin worked for a software company in St. Petersburg, Russia, before he applied his computer skills to grand theft, devising ways to rob American banks from his home computer. Beginning in July 1994, Levin cracked Citibank's computer network and transferred funds to bank accounts in California, Finland, Israel, Germany, the Netherlands, and Switzerland. Within three months, through 40 transfers, he stole $10.7 million.

Citibank's security system flagged two August transfers—totaling $330,800—as "strange," tracing them to a pair of San Francisco companies owned by a friend of Levin's, Jevgenij Korolkov. After preliminary questioning, Korolkov fled the country and the thefts continued, but investigators soon identified Levin and broadcast his description to police worldwide. Five cohorts in other countries were jailed at the time of Levin's arrest in England. Citibank claimed that all but $400,000 of the stolen money was recovered.

Levin's attorneys stalled his extradition until July 1997, when he was flown to New York for trial. On February 24, 1998, he pled guilty to a single count of conspiring to steal $3.7 million. The court imposed a three-year prison term and ordered Levin to repay $240,015.

VIRTUAL CRIME

In bygone years, bank robbers had to risk their lives and freedom stealing cash at gunpoint. Many still do—the FBI recorded 1,569 traditional bank holdups in the last three months of 2007 alone, with losses of $24.5 million[1]—but a new breed of felon loots banks and commits other serious crimes without leaving the comforts of home.

Cybercrimes are not limited to long-distance looting of banks. Other common offenses include identify theft, "hacking" of restricted systems, forgery, fraud, extortion, harassment, money-laundering, and distribution of child pornography. In 2007 the Internet Crime Complaint Center (ICCC) received 219,533 complaints of alleged cybercrime, referring 90,008 cases to local, state, and federal authorities for further investigation. The ICCC calculated losses from computer fraud at $239.09 million (an average of $680 per victim), up from $198.44 million in 2006.[2]

As usual throughout history, criminals recognized the potential of computers before law enforcement caught up to the trend. As this book went to press, only 26 of America's 50 states had laws defining cybercrime. The federal government was quicker to react, pursuing offenders under statutes that include the Computer Fraud and Abuse Act (1986), Electronic Communications Privacy Act (1986), Economic Espionage Act (1996), No Electronic Theft ("NET") Act (1997), Digital Millennium Copyright Act (1998), Identity Theft and Assumption Deterrence Act (1998), and the CAN-SPAM Act (2003).

COMPUTER FRAUD

Fraud consists of lying to induce some action by another person which benefits the liar or some other party to the victim's detriment. Cyberfraud takes several forms, including unauthorized alteration of computer input;

alteration or destruction of computer output to hide illegal transactions; manipulation of stored data; and false commercial offers including financial transactions and merchandise sales. Common examples include:

Advance-fee fraud. These frauds began in 1992, with e-mails transmitted from Africa, Asia, and Eastern Europe, later expanding to cover the planet. Typically, an e-mail from a stranger offers the recipient a fortune in return for help with some problem that requires the victim to spend money in advance. The usual tale involves splitting the proceeds from a huge bank account, inheritance, or lottery payoff if the victim first pays certain fees or expenses. A variation, known as the "Spanish prisoner scam," requests money to bribe prison guards for the release of a (fictitious) wealthy inmate, who will then deliver part of his (nonexistent) fortune. Losses reportedly amount to hundreds of millions of dollars per year.[3]

Dating scams. Online dating is a vast industry, and thieves have infested the market from its beginning. So-called sweetheart swindles involve the virtual seduction of lonely victims by strangers who promise romance in exchange for money. The scams differ from prostitution since those who part with cash rarely, if ever, meet their supposed soul mates. While some online relationships have happy endings, sweetheart scams are characterized by strangers who profess love quickly, then ask for money to cash checks, defray medical bills, support business ventures, or travel to meet their "new love." Sexy photos often serve as bait, but the seductive correspondents vanish with their victims' cash.

Ticket fraud. Another common cyberswindle involves sale of tickets to popular concerts, shows, and sporting events. Gullible buyers send money or pay by credit card (paving the way for future thefts), but then receive worthless counterfeit tickets or none at all. One large-scale example involved the global sale of tickets to the 2008 Beijing Olympic Games through a Web site established by the U.S.-registered company Xclusive Leisure and Hospitality. By August 4, 2008, sales of fake tickets exceeded $50 million.[4]

CYBERTHEFT

Some criminals lack the patience to correspond with potential victims. They prefer immediate results, obtained by thefts of cash direct from bank accounts or automatic tellers, use of stolen credit card numbers to purchase high-ticket items, or hijacking of a victim's life itself.

When theft is mentioned, people most often think of losing money or personal property, such as a vehicle, handbag, or items stolen from a home. In fact, however, some criminals specialize in *identity theft,* stealing a victim's name and personal information (Social Security numbers, numbers for credit or debit cards, bank accounts, insurance policies, etc.) and using that data to pose as the victim while stealing him blind. Identity thieves commonly run up huge credit card bills, empty their victims' bank accounts, or purchase items such as cars and homes. Such crimes destroy the victim's credit rating, leaving those who have been robbed to prove that they did not authorize the transactions. Victims seldom recover all of their stolen money, and expensive legal cases may be required to get any.

Vladimir Levin's case illustrates the danger of computer *bank robbery,* but he was by no means the only practitioner. Nearly 2 million Americans suffered raids on their checking accounts by cyberthieves between June 2003 and June 2004, and some of the thefts are quite large.[5] In 2006 a Russian hacker known as "The Corpse" invaded the computer system of Sweden's Nordea Bank to steal $1 million from depositors. Altogether, various thieves robbed the accounts of 250 Nordea customers during a 15-month period.[6] One month after those losses were revealed, in February 2007, police in Izmir, Turkey, arrested 17 members of a gang that hacked Internet bank accounts and stole $300,000. Authorities claimed that Russian hackers sold the thieves login data for thousands of Turkish depositors before the raids began.[7]

CRIMES AGAINST CHILDREN

Despite some attempts to regulate Internet content, including passage of strict laws forbidding production, sale, or possession of child pornography, the illegal industry thrives. Pornography of all kinds generated sales exceeding $97 billion worldwide in 2006, with an estimated $4.9 billion from online sales. Each second of every day, an estimated 28,528 Internet users view pornographic images. At least 100,000 Web sites offer illegal child pornography for viewing at a price.[8]

Against that tide, law enforcement wages nonstop campaigns to identify and prosecute the producers, vendors, and recipients of child pornography. Some of those efforts include:

Operation Cathedral, an international campaign targeting an Internet child porn ring called the Wonderland Club. On September 1, 1998, officers in 12 countries arrested 107 suspects and confiscated computers containing 750,000 illegal images. Seven British defendants were convicted on multiple charges in 2001.[9]

Operation Avalanche, launched across the United States in 1999, climaxed with 144 arrests in August 2001. The operation took its name from a child-porn Web site called Landslide.[10]

Operation Ore, an international campaign, began in 1999 and identified 7,250 suspects. In Britain alone, police searched 4,283 homes and arrested 3,744 alleged offenders. Of those, 1,848

INNOCENT IMAGES

While investigating a Maryland child's disappearance in May 1993, FBI agents identified two suspects with a 25-year record of exploiting minors. Further pursuit of that case revealed that many pedophiles transmit child pornography via computers and use e-mails or chat rooms to entrap children in sexual activity. In 1995 the FBI launched its Innocent Images National Initiative (IINI), targeting groups and individuals who exploit children for sex or profit, including producers and purchasers of child pornography.

Between 1996 and 2007, agents assigned to the IINI conducted 20,134 investigations, resulting in 9,469 arrests, and 6,863 convictions or plea-bargains.[14] Four suspects investigated under the IINI have been listed as fugitives on the bureau's Ten Most Wanted list. They include:

Eric Franklin Rosser, listed in December 2000 on charges of producing and distributing child pornography, including videotapes of himself molesting an 11-year-old girl in Thailand.

were charged, 1,451 were convicted, and 493 others escaped with warnings from the court. Another 35 suspects committed suicide, while police removed 140 children from homes deemed dangerous.[11]

Operation Amethyst, a drive carried out by Irish police in April 2004, based on information obtained from the U.S. Postal Service. The 130 persons arrested included a judge and celebrity chef Tim Allen (who was sentenced to 240 hours of community service after donating $62,000 to charity).[12]

Operation Auxin was executed by Australian authorities in September 2004. The 130 defendants had purchased child porn from a Web site run by Belarusian gangsters, with credit card charges processed through a company in Florida.[13]

Operation Predator, initiated by U.S. Immigration and Customs Enforcement in July 2003, continues to the present day. By Janu-

Arrested in Bangkok on August 21, 2001, Rosser was extradited to America and received a 16-year sentence in October 2003.

Michael Scott Bliss, listed in January 2002 as a fugitive from child-molestation charges in Vermont. Bliss videotaped his abuse of a nine-year-old girl and posted copies on the Internet. Captured in Los Angeles on April 23, 2002, Bliss received a 22-year prison term in February 2004.

Richard Steve Goldberg, listed in June 2002 for molesting several young girls in California and photographing the assaults. Canadian police arrested Goldberg in May 2007 and returned him to America for trial. He pled guilty in December 2007 and received a 20-year sentence.

Jon Savarino Schillaci, listed in September 2007 and still at large as this book went to press. Schillaci is charged with molesting a New Hampshire boy in 1999 and fleeing the state to avoid prosecution. He is an ex-convict who served time on previous child-molestation charges and met his last known victim while corresponding with the child's parents from prison.

David L. Smith, creator of the "Melissa" virus, leaves the Monmouth County Courthouse in Freehold, New Jersey, after his first court appearance in April 1999. He later agreed to a plea bargain and received a 20-month sentence and a $5,000 fine. *AP Photo/Daniel Hulshizer*

ary 2007, the campaign had produced more than 9,300 arrests. Of the pedophiles identified, 5,000 were immigrants whose crimes resulted in deportation.[15]

Operation Pin, a collaborative effort by the Virtual Global Task-force, including agents of the FBI, Interpol, the Royal Canadian Mounted Police (RCMP), Britain's National Crime Squad, and the Australian Federal Police. The campaign to trap pedophiles with "honeypot" Web sites resembling child porn outlets began in December 2003. While no arrest statistics are available, the task force claimed to have rescued 31 children from abusive situations by June 2007.[16]

GARY MCKINNON

Between February 2001 and March 2002 a hacker calling himself "Solo" penetrated 97 Web sites operated by the U.S. Army, Navy, Air Force, and Department of Defense, as well as the National Aeronautics and Space Administration. In one case, soon after the terrorist attacks of September 11, 2001, he hacked computers at a naval air station to alter and delete critical files, thus rendering security systems inoperable. The cost of tracking and correcting problems caused by Solo was approximately $700,000.[17]

Officers of Britain's National Hi-Tech Crime Unit identified Solo as Gary McKinnon, a 36-year-old Scotsman employed as a computer systems administrator. They threatened to file charges under England's Computer Misuse Act, but prosecutors dropped the case after McKinnon claimed that he was merely seeking evidence of visitors from outer space and did not mean to sabotage the military sites. American prosecutors then indicted him for perpetrating what they called "the biggest military computer hack of all time," but McKinnon resisted extradition.[18] In April 2007, the High Court of London ordered him transported to America, but his lawyers appealed to the House of Lords, where the extradition verdict was affirmed on July 30, 2008. McKinnon appealed that judgment, but the appeal was rejected in July 2009. The appeals process continued as of this writing. If convicted, McKinnon faces a maximum sentence of 70 years in prison.

CYBERTERRORISM

Cyberterrorism is defined as any terroristic act involving computers. Examples range from Internet threats of impending violence to hacking of government or commercial networks, online harassment of specific groups or individuals, computer raids on bank accounts to finance terrorist activities, and collection of personal data for use in blackmail.

While no documented cases of organized cyberterrorism have been publicized, officials in nations around the world take the threat seriously. In November 2008, Pakistan's President Asif Ali Zardari signed a new Prevention of Electronic Crimes Ordinance which mandates execution or life imprisonment for cyberterrorists whose actions result in death. Nonfatal offenses carry a penalty of 10 years' imprisonment and a fine equivalent to $128,000.[19]

Justice Department spokesmen cite two famous cases as examples of what cyberterrorists *might* do, if given the chance. In March 1999 a computer worm called "Melissa," written by New Jersey resident David Smith and named for a stripper he met on vacation in Florida, spread like wildfire through self-generating e-mails. Each time a new computer was infected, the worm sent copies of itself to 50 addresses from the user's e-mail address book, without the victim-user's knowledge. More computers were thus infected, and so on, until various systems were clogged with infected e-mails. As a result, North American corporations suffered damages of $80 million. FBI agents and New Jersey State Police officers traced Smith, charging him with multiple counts of computer fraud and abuse. Facing 40 years in prison, Smith pled guilty to one reduced charge and received a 20-month sentence, with a $5,000 fine.[20]

In February 2000 a Canadian hacker who called himself "MafiaBoy" launched denial-of-service attacks against several commercial Web sites including Yahoo!, Amazon.com, CNN, Dell, and eBay. During the three-hour ordeal, Yahoo! alone was flooded with "spam" at a rate of one gigabyte per second. Investigators placed total damages at $1.2 billion. FBI and RCMP agents were baffled until 15-year-old Michael Calce boasted of his crime in various Internet chat rooms. Although charged with 54 counts of illegal computer access and 10 counts of malicious mischief, Calce escaped with eight months of "open custody," a year's probation, and court-imposed restrictions on Internet access.[21]

Punishing Crime

Starke, Florida

Inmates at Florida's state prison call the electric chair "Old Sparky." The reason was clear on May 4, 1990, when flames erupted from inmate Jesse Tafero's scalp during his execution. Investigators blamed the problem on "inadvertent human error," specifically substitution of a synthetic sponge for a damp natural sponge normally placed beneath the electrode strapped to a prisoner's head.[1]

Seven years later, an identical accident occurred during the execution of Pedro Medina, clouding the death chamber with smoke. This time, prison officials blamed the fire on a corroded copper screen in Old Sparky's headpiece, but independent experts reported that prison guards had once again failed to apply the sponge properly. In January 2000, state lawmakers changed Florida's mode of execution to "painless" lethal injection. Nonetheless, executioners took 33 minutes to find a vein on their first attempt, with Bennie Demps, in June 2000. In his final statement, Demps declared, "They butchered me back there."[2]

JUSTICE OR REVENGE?

Punishment of criminals has preoccupied human society since ancient times, with methods ranging from small fines and public embarrassment to imprisonment, torture, mutilation, and death. Each civilization prioritized crime, deciding which offenses deserved the worst punishment, commonly based on social customs or religious beliefs. An act

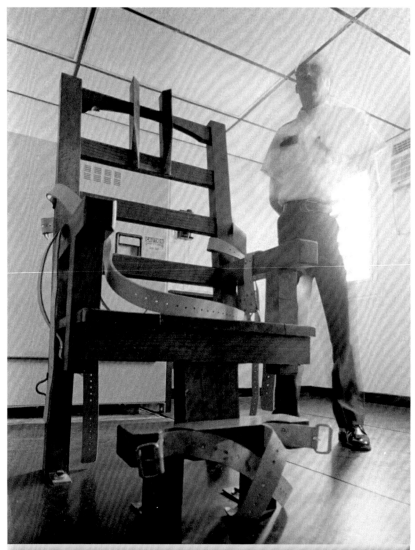

A guard at Florida State Prison stands by Florida's notorious electric chair, "Old Sparky." Pedro Medina was executed in a fiery electrocution in the same chair on March 25, 1997. *AP Photo/Mark Foley, File*

that might be legal in one country could rate whipping in another or execution in a third.

Early Americans inherited their views on crime and punishment from their respective homelands. British colonists combined Old Testament rules with England's Common Law, while adding new twists to suit life on the American frontier. Nonfatal punishments included banishment, placement of offenders in the stocks or pillory (where they were often pelted with rotten fruit), public whipping, branding, cropping of ears, or boring of tongues with hot irons (for convicted blasphemers). Shaming was also popular, as when adulterers were forced to wear a letter "A" sewn on their clothing, while counterfeiters wore a "C." Failure to pay a debt meant prison time until the 1830s, and modified versions of debtors' prison continue today, with incarceration of parents who dodge child-support and convicted offenders who cannot pay fines.

Colonial trials were shorter than modern proceedings. No lawyers were present, and judges often rendered verdicts without a jury, after hearing witnesses. Unfortunately, some judges acted more like prosecutors and were clearly prejudiced against defendants, especially in cases like the Salem witch trials, where ministers filed the charges *and* served as trial judges.

BEHIND BARS

Before the American Revolution (1775-83), towns ran their own jails for local offenders, but no larger prisons existed. Later, various states constructed penitentiaries (from the Latin *pænitentia,* "repentance") to house lawbreakers. New York's Auburn Prison, built in 1816, employed harsh punishment, hard-labor details, and a strict code of silence. Pennsylvania's Eastern State Penitentiary, built in 1829, held convicts in solitary confinement but gave them personal gardens and workshops.

Conflicting tendencies toward punishment and rehabilitation persist today. The 1870s witnessed a movement to transform prisons into "reformatories," which would educate offenders and mold them into useful citizens. The "science" of penology (prison administration) inspired some wardens to ban whipping and other forms of corporal punishment, while others continued using torture sanctioned by state law. Arkansas permitted whipping of prisoners until the early 1970s.

The civil rights movement of the 1960s included legal recognition of certain basic rights for prison inmates, but rising crime rates in the same decade produced a backlash from the 1970s onward, with calls

THE ROCK

Explorer Juan Manuel de Ayala charted San Francisco Bay in 1775 and named Alcatraz Island for the pelicans (*alcatraces* in Spanish) he found nesting there. The U.S. Army fortified Alcatraz in 1853, then converted it to a military prison in 1868. By 1898 the cell blocks housed 450 prisoners, surrounded by shark-infested waters that discouraged escapes. Construction enlarged the prison between 1909 and 1912, in time to receive conscientious objectors during World War I.

Alcatraz Island, now part of the Golden State National Recreation Area, was home to a legendary prison before the facility was shut down in March 1963. *AP Photo/Mike Stewart*

for "zero tolerance," mandatory minimum sentencing, adult trials for minors, and elimination of early release. The net result was a huge increase in America's convict population, with debatable impact on national crime rates.

In June 2007 a total of 2,299,116 prisoners were confined in U.S. jails and prisons—an average of 509 per 100,000 Americans, or 957 per 100,000 American males. Totals included 2,090,800 male inmates and 208,300 females. Racial disparities were evident in the statistics. While Caucasians accounted for 74 percent of the population, they

The Department of Justice acquired Alcatraz in October 1933, as part of Washington's first "war on crime," and the island received its first federal prisoners in August 1934. Nicknamed "The Rock," Alcatraz housed some of America's most notorious "public enemies" from the 1930s, including "Scarface" Al Capone, George "Machine Gun" Kelly, Alvin "Old Creepy" Karpis, and several members of Detroit's Purple Gang. Despite his famous nickname, Robert Stroud, the "Birdman of Alcatraz," actually raised and sold birds at Leavenworth prison, before his transfer to The Rock in 1942.

Alcatraz officials claim that no prisoners ever escaped from the island. Thirty-six tried, of whom seven were shot and two drowned. In May 1946, an escape attempt by six inmates sparked the "Battle of Alcatraz," suppressed by U.S. Marines at a cost of five dead and 12 wounded. Three other inmates vanished in June 1962, while trying to escape on homemade rafts. Authorities believe they drowned, but the case inspired Clint Eastwood's film *Escape from Alcatraz* (1979).

Attorney General Robert Kennedy closed Alcatraz in March 1963, citing high operating costs. Members of the American Indian Movement occupied Alcatraz for several weeks in 1969, protesting government treatment of Native Americans. In 1973 The Rock became a national recreation area, accessible to tourists.

comprised only 37 percent of those incarcerated. Hispanics, at 14.8 percent overall, comprised 19.2 percent of all inmates. African Americans, with 13.4 percent of the U.S. population, comprised 38 percent of U.S. prisoners.[3]

By April 2008 the United States, with only 5 percent of the world's population, held nearly one-fourth of all prisoners confined on Earth. One in every 100 American adults was incarcerated for some offense, or 751 per 100,000 residents (including children). The next-closest industrialized nation was Russia, with 651 prisoners per 100,000 population, while England had 151 per 100,000, Germany had 88 per 100,000, and Japan had 63 per 100,000 incarcerated. China, with four times America's population, had 1.6 million prisoners, compared to America's 2.3 million.[4]

What affect does widespread imprisonment have on crime rates? According to the FBI, while America's census and prison population grew steadily from 1988 to 2007, the number of reported violent crimes rose and fell as follows:[5]

1988 – 1,566,221	1998 – 1,533,887
1989 – 1,646,037	1999 – 1,426,044
1990 – 1,820,127	2000 – 1,425,486
1991 – 1,911,767	2001 – 1,439,480
1992 – 1,932,274	2002 – 1,423,677
1993 – 1,926,017	2003 – 1,383,676
1994 – 1,857,670	2004 – 1,360,088
1995 – 1,798,792	2005 – 1,390,745
1996 – 1,688,540	2006 – 1,418,043
1997 – 1,636,096	2007 – 1,408,337

If prisons were expected to reform inmates, they clearly failed. In June 2002, the Bureau of Justice Statistics reported findings from a survey of 272,211 prisoners released from prisons in 15 states during 1994. Overall, 67.5 percent were rearrested for a new crime within three years, 46.9 percent were convicted, and 25.4 percent received new prison terms. Another 26.4 percent returned to prison for violating terms of their parole. In terms of crimes committed, 61.7 percent of violent offenders returned to prison for new violent crimes (including 40.7 percent for a second homicide); 73.8 returned for new property crimes (theft, fraud, or arson); 66.7 percent returned for new drug offenses; and 62.2 percent returned for new public-order offenses (drunk driving, vice, or weapons charges). Nearly two-thirds of those rearrested went back to prison within their first year of freedom.[6]

CAPITAL PUNISHMENT

Execution remains the most controversial form of criminal punishment, in America and around the world. At least 15,583 prisoners were executed between 1608 and 2008, within the present-day United States.[7] Debate surrounds the morality and humanity of capital punishment, as well as the question of wrongful convictions condemning innocent persons.

Execution ranks among the oldest criminal punishments practiced on Earth. The Old Testament books of Genesis through Deuteronomy imposed death for a wide variety of acts, ranging from murder and kidnapping to blasphemy, false prophecy, witchcraft, perjury, profaning the Sabbath, worshiping "false gods," striking or cursing one's parents, and various sexual offenses. Many of those penalties made the leap to European and early American law, while other capital crimes were added. By the eighteenth century, British statutes listed 222 capital offenses, including most kinds of theft, "being in the company of Gypsies for one month," and "strong evidence of malice in a child aged 7–14 years of age." Many of those laws were repealed in the 1800s, but execution of British murderers continued until 1965. By November 2008, 93 countries had banned capital punishment, nine used it only in "special circumstances," and 35 with existing death penalty laws had executed no one in 10 years. Sixty nations, including the United States, continue executions today, although 24 states have discarded the death penalty.[8]

Critics of capital punishment argue that executions are cruel, regardless of the method used, and that America is out of step with the majority of modern industrial nations in performing executions. They also cite the possibility of wrongful convictions claiming innocent lives. Since 2000, 225 American prison inmates from 33 states have been cleared of all charges by DNA testing, which did not exist at the time of their trials. Seventeen of those inmates faced execution when they were exonerated, and abolitionists claim that other innocents have been put to death. In January 2003, faced with evidence of "frame-ups" by corrupt police and prosecutors, Illinois Governor George Ryan commuted the death sentences of 167 condemned prisoners.[9]

Supporters of capital punishment defend their position on moral, economic, and emotional grounds. Many base their support on the Bible, though few suggest a return to the days of executing sassy children or witches. They argue that Exodus 21:23-25 demands "life for life, eye for eye, tooth for tooth, hand for hand, foot for foot, burn for burn, wound for wound," yet they accept imprisonment for any crime but murder, without proposing torture or mutilation for lesser offenses.

Economic arguments in favor of death suggest that it is cheaper to execute killers than to jail them for life, but government auditors disagree. In Maryland, capital murder trials cost an average $470,000 more than noncapital trials, and capital appeals cost $100,000 more than appeals of prison terms. California's Commission on the Fair Administration of Justice reported in June 2008 that the average yearly cost for housing life-term prisoners is $90,000 each, while death row inmates cost the state $204,478 each. In New Jersey, 197 capital trials

FURMAN V. GEORGIA (1972)

On the night of August 11, 1967, William Micke surprised a burglar in the act of robbing his home in Savannah, Georgia. The intruder, William Furman, tried to flee but tripped and fell, accidentally firing his pistol. The bullet killed Micke, resulting in a murder charge against Furman. Jurors convicted him at a one-day trial in September 1968, and Furman was sentenced to die. Four years later, the United States Supreme Court combined Furman's case with those of death-row inmates Elmer Branch and Lucius Jackson, condemned for rape in Texas and Georgia, respectively. The court's decision in those cases, collectively titled *Furman v. Georgia*, had a dramatic impact on American rules for capital punishment.

Noting that all three defendants were African Americans, the Supreme Court ruled that existing death penalty statutes throughout the nation violated the U.S. Constitution's Eighth-Amendment ban on "cruel and unusual" punishment and the Fourteenth Amendment's guarantee of "equal protection" under law. Justice Potter Stewart wrote, for the majority: "These death sentences are cruel and unusual in the same way that being struck by lightning is cruel and unusual. For, of all the people convicted of rapes and murders in 1967 and 1968, many just as reprehensible as these, the petitioners are among a capriciously selected random handful upon whom

produced 60 death sentences at a cost of $1.3 million per case between 1983 and 2005, with 50 sentences reversed on appeal and no executions performed. In Tennessee, capital trials cost 48 percent more than trials in which prosecutors seek life prison terms. Each execution in North Carolina costs $2.16 million more than housing an inmate for life. Florida executions cost an average $24 million each from 1976 to 2000.[13]

Finally come the emotional arguments that killers deserve to die, and that they may escape from custody—or even be paroled—to kill again if they survive. While each person must make his own judgment

---

the sentence of death has in fact been imposed. My concurring Brothers have demonstrated that, if any basis can be discerned for the selection of these few to be sentenced to death, it is the constitutionally impermissible basis of race....I simply conclude that the Eighth and Fourteenth Amendments cannot tolerate the infliction of a sentence of death under legal systems that permit this unique penalty to be so wantonly and so freakishly imposed."[10]

Four justices, all appointed by President Richard Nixon, dissented from the court's decision on grounds that capital punishment had been deemed acceptable throughout Anglo-American legal history. Nonetheless, *Furman v. Georgia* overturned death sentences imposed on 587 defendants from coast to coast, including one condemned in 1958. Of those, 322 were subsequently released from prison.[11]

After *Furman*, lawmakers in 37 states passed new death penalty statutes. Those laws restrict capital punishment to cases of murder, generally accompanied by "special circumstances" such as torture, murder for hire, multiple slayings, or murder of a police officer. The Supreme Court approved those new guidelines in *Gregg v. Georgia* (1976), and American executions resumed in January 1977, when a Utah firing squad shot double-murderer Gary Gilmore. By October 2008 a total of 1,123 inmates had been executed under the new rules for capital punishment.[12]

on who "deserves" to live, statistics for the re-arrest of violent ex-convicts fuel the fear that paroled slayers may kill again if released.

No record exists of any American prisoner sentenced to life without parole being released, except where innocence was subsequently proved by DNA or other scientific evidence, but prisoners *do* escape. The Bureau of Justice Statistics reports 14,305 escapes from state prisons in 1993, declining to 6,530 (out of 1.1 million inmates) in 1998. The Association of State Correctional Administrators cites a more dramatic drop spanning two decades, from 12.4 escapes per 1,000 inmates in 1981 to .5 per 1,000 in 2001. Florida authorities lost 122 prisoners between June 2005 and June 2006, but none escaped from inside prison walls, and 55 percent were recaptured within 24 hours, 92 percent within 12 months.[14]

Such figures offer no consolation to those who fear killers invading their homes. Anxiety and anger spawned by crime ensure that debates over capital punishment, gun control, and related topics will continue with no end in sight.

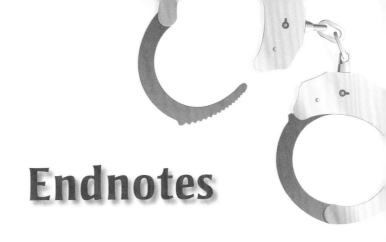

Endnotes

Introduction

1. W. G. Macpherson, W. B. Leishman and S. L. Cummins, *Official Medical History of the War—Pathology* (London: His Majesty's Stationery Office, 1923).
2. U.S. National Archives, "Statistical information about casualties of the Vietnam Conflict," http://www.archives.gov/research/vietnam-war/casualty-statistics.html.
3. David Chalmers, *Backfire: How the Ku Klux Klan Helped the Civil Rights Movement* (Lanham, Md.: Rowman & Littlefield, 2003), 97–106.
4. FBI, "FBI Uniform Crime Reports," http://www.fbi.gov/ucr/ucr.htm; National Counterterrorism Center, *Worldwide Incidents Tracking System*, http://wits.nctc.gov (Accessed November 5, 2008).

Chapter 1

1. "The Homicide Report," *Los Angeles Times,* http://latimesblogs.latimes.com/homicidereport (Accessed November 5, 2008).
2. Sean Cockerham, "Begich lead increases in race for Senate," *Anchorage Daily News*, November 14, 2008.
3. Yu Le, "China milk victims may have reached 94,000," Reuters, http://www.marlerclark.com/case_news/detail/china-milk-victims-may-have-reached-94000 (Posted October 8, 2008).
4. Barbara Demick, "China milk scandal hits home," *Los Angeles Times,* September 27, 2008; CNN, "Tainted milk deaths rise in China," CNN.com, http://www.cnn.com/2008/WORLD/asiapcf/12/01/china.milk/ (December 2, 2008).
5. FBI, "FBI Uniform Crime Reports," http://www.fbi.gov/ucr/cius2007/index.html (Accessed November 5, 2008).
6. U.S. Fire Administration, "Intentionally Set Structure Fires," http://www.usfa.dhs.gov/statistics/arson (Accessed November 5, 2008).
7. Bureau of Justice Statistics, http://www.ojp.usdoj.gov/bjs/intimate/ipv.htm (Accessed November 5, 2008).
8. U.S. Dept. of Health and Human Services, http://www.acf.hhs.gov/programs/cb/pubs/cm06/index.htm; Bureau of Justice Statistics, http://www.ojp.usdoj.gov/bjs/intimate/ipv.htm (Accessed November 5, 2008).
9. Bill Dedman, "Deadly Lessons: School Shooters Tell Why," *Chicago Sun-Times*, October 15, 2000.

10. Bureau of Justice Statistics, http://www.ojp.usdoj.gov/bjs/intimate/ipv.htm.
11. FBI, "FBI History," http://www.fbi.gov/libref/historic/history/new deal.htm (Accessed November 5, 2008).
12. Drug Sense, "Drug War Clock," http://www.drugsense.org/wod clock.htm (Accessed August 26, 2009); Bureau of Justice Statistics, http://www.ojp.usdoj.gov/bjs/prisons.htm (Accessed August 26, 2009).
13. United Nations Office on Drugs and Crime, *World Drug Report 2008* (Vienna, Austria: United Nations, 2008), 45.
14. National Institute on Drug Abuse, "InfoFacts: Crack and Cocaine," http://www.nida.nih.gov/infofacts/cocaine.html (Accessed August 26, 2009).
15. Office of National Drug Control Policy, *The Price and Purity of Illicit Drugs: 1981 Through the Second Quarter of 2003* (Washington D.C.: Executive Office of the President, 2004), 62–63.
16. Gary Fields, "White House czar calls for end to 'war on drugs,'"
17. National Center for Education Statistics, http://nces.ed.gov/programs/crimeindicators/ crime indicators2007 (Accessed November 5, 2008).
18. Rape, Abuse & Incest National Network, http://www.rainn.org/statistics (Accessed November 5, 2008).
19. FBI Uniform Crime Reports, http://www.fbi.gov/ucr/cius2007/data/table_09.html (Accessed November 5, 2008). *Wall Street Journal,* May 14, 2009.
20. "Discounting Hate," *Southern Poverty Law Center's Intelligence Report* (Winter 2001): 6-15.
21. William Turner, *Hoover's FBI* (New York: Thunder's Mouth Press, 1993), 249–257.
22. Mark Ames, *Going Postal* (New York: Soft Skull Press, 2005).
23. Bureau of Justice Statistics, http://www.ojp.usdoj.gov/bjs/intimate/ipv.htm and http://www.ojp.usdoj.gov/bjs/pub/pdf/wv96.pdf (Accessed November 5, 2008).
24. ADT Security Services, "Shoplifting Costs U.S. Retailers $40.5 Billion According to ADT-Sponsored Survey," Tyco PRNewswire, http://tyco.mediaroom.com/index.php?s= 43&item=20 (Posted December 4, 2007); and Shoplifting Statistics & Tactics, http://www.associatedcontent.com /article/183545/shoplifting_statistics_tactics_ 75_of.html?cat=47 (Accessed November 5, 2008).
25. American Management Association, *Crimes Against Business Project: Background, Findings and Recommendations* (New York: AMA, 1977).
26. "Archbishop Paul Marcinkus," *Times Online,* http://www.timesonline.co.uk/tol/comment/obituaries/article733405.ece, (Posted February 22, 2006).

Chapter 2

1. NationMaster.com "John Billington," NationMaster.com http://www.nationmaster.com/encyclopedia/John-Billington (Accessed September 29, 2009).
2. Death Penalty Information Center, "Executions in the U.S. 1608–2002," deathpenaltyinfo.org,

http://www.deathpenaltyinfo.org/ESPYyear.pdf (Accessed November 6, 2008); Hugh Graham and Ted Gurr, *The History of Violence in America* (New York: Bantam, 1969), 218–226; National Law Enforcement Officers Memorial Fund, http://www.nleomf.com/TheMemorial/Facts/year.htm (Accessed November 6, 2008).

3. "Casualties in the Civil War," Shotgun's Home of the American Civil War, http://www.civilwarhome.com/casualties.htm (Accessed November 6, 2008).

4. Allen Trelease, *White Terror* (New York: Harper & Row, 1971), 135.

5. "Dates that Individual States Enacted Prohibition Laws," Pre-Pro.com, http://www.pre-pro.com/dry_states.htm (Accessed November 6, 2008).

6. Marc Carlson, "Historical Witches and Witchtrials in North America," http://www.personal.utulsa.edu/~Marc-Carlson/witchtrial/na.html (Accessed November 6, 2008).

7. Henry Lee, *How Dry We Were* (Englewood Cliffs, N.J.: Prentice-Hall, 1963), 6, 68.

8. William Helmer and Rick Mattix, *Public Enemies* (New York: Checkmark, 1998), 65, 292–303; John Kobler, *Ardent Spirits* (New York: G.P. Putnam's Sons, 1973), 293.

9. Lee, 162; Herbert Asbury, *The Great Illusion* (Westport, Conn.: Greenwood, 1950), 177, 185; Richard Lindberg, *To Serve and Collect* (Carbondale, Ill.: Southern Illinois University Press, 1991), 169.

10. Helmer and Mattix, 65; Kobler, 283; Lee, 156–157; Charles Merz,

The Dry Decade (Seattle: University of Washington Press, 1930), 183–187.

11. Bureau of Justice Statistics, http://www.ojp.usdoj.gov/bjs/dcf/enforce.htm (Accessed November 6, 2008).

12. Bureau of Justice Statistics, http://www.ojp.usdoj.gov/bjs/pub/pdf/p06.pdf (Accessed November 6, 2008).

13. American Gaming Association, http://www.americangaming.org/Industry/state/statistics.cfm?stateid=0 (Accessed November 6, 2008).

14. "Nevada brothels want to be good neighbor," MSNBC, May 10, 2005; Corey Levitan, "Stark Raving Madam," *Las Vegas Review Journal*, July 7, 2008.

15. Dan Bilefsky, "Belgian Experiment," *Wall Street Journal*, May 26, 2005.

16. Janice G. Raymond, "Health effects of prostitution," *Making the Harm Visible*, http://www.uri.edu/artsci/wms/hughes/mhvhealt.htm (Accessed August 26, 2009).

17. Drug War Facts, "Annual Causes of Death in the United States," http://drugwarfacts.org/cms/?q=node/30 (Accessed August 26, 2009).

Chapter 3

1. FBI Uniform Crime Reports, http://www.fbi.gov/ucr/cius2007/data/table_07.html (Accessed November 8, 2008).

2. Lawrence Bergreen, *Capone: The Man and the Era* (New York: Touchstone, 1994), 589–590.

3. John Douglas, Ann Burgess, Allen Burgess, and Robert Ressler,

Crime Classification Manual (San Francisco: Josey-Bass, 199?), 20–21.

4. Douglas et al., 20.

5. Michael Newton, *The Encyclopedia of Serial Killers* (New York: Facts on File, 2000), 78.

6. FBI Uniform Crime Reports, http://www.fbi.gov/ucr/cius2007/data/table_20.html (Accessed November 8, 2008); Suicide Statistics, http://www.suicide.org/suicide-statistics.html#2005 (Accessed November 8, 2008); National Safety Council, *Deaths Due to Unintentional Injuries 2000* (Itasca, Ill.: NSC, 2001), 8–9, 84; Edward C. Klatt, "Firearms Tutorial," The University of Utah Eccles Health Sciences Library, http://library.med.utah.edu/WebPath/TUTORIAL/GUNS/ GUNSTAT.html (Accessed November 8, 2008).

7. National Rifle Association Institute for Legislative Action, "Compendium of State Firearm Laws," NRA-ILA.org, http://www.nraila.org/GunLaws/Federal /Read.aspx?id=74.

8. "How often are firearms used in self defense?" GunCite, http://www.guncite.com/gun_control_gcdguse.htm (Accessed November 8, 2008).

9. Thomas Page, "The Real Judge Lynch," *Atlantic Monthly* (December 1901): 731–743.

10. "1959 Tuskegee Institute Lynch Report," *Montgomery* (Ala.) *Advertiser*, April 26, 1959; Lynching Statistics, http://faculty.berea.edu/browners/chesnutt/classroom/lynchingstat.html (Accessed November 8, 2008); The Lynching Century, http://www.geocities.com/Colosseum/Base/8507/NLists.htm (Accessed November 8, 2008).

11. Barry Yeoman, "Soldiers of Good Fortune," *Mother Jones*, http://www.motherjones.com/news/feature/2003/05/ma_365_01.html (Posted June 1, 2003).

12. Steve Fainaru, "How Blackwater sniper fire felled 3 Iraqi guards," *Washington Post*, November 8, 2007.

13. John Broder, "Ex-paratrooper is suspect in a Blackwater killing," *New York Times,* October 3, 2007.

14. James Glanz and Sabrina Tavernise, "Security firm faces criminal charges in Iraq," *New York Times,* http://www.nytimes.com/2007/09/23/world/middleeast/23blackwater.html (September 23, 2007).

15. David Johnston and John Broder, "FBI says guards killed 14 Iraqis without cause," *New York Times,* November 14, 2007; "Iraq to end contractor immunity," BBC News, http://news.bbc.co.uk/2/hi/middle_east/7069173.stm (Accessed August 28, 2009).

16. Warren Strobel, "Blackwater faces fine for illegally shipping arms to Iraq," *Boston Herald*, November 13, 2008.

17. Office of Juvenile Justice and Delinquency Prevention, http://www.ncjrs.gov/ pdffiles1/ojjdp/fs200203.pdf .

18. National Criminal Justice Reference Center, http://www.ncjrs.gov/spotlight/ gangs/facts.html (Accessed November 8, 2008).

19. LAPD Gang Statistics, http://www.lapdonline.org/top_ten_most_

wanted_gang_members/
content_basic_view/24435
(Accessed November 8, 2008).

20. Department of Justice, "About prison gangs," http://www.usdoj. gov/criminal/gangunit/about / prisongangs.html (Accessed November 8, 2008).

21. Department of Justice, "Motorcycle Gangs," http://www.usdoj. gov/criminal/gangunit/gangs/ motorcycle.html (Accessed September 29, 2009); "Biker gangs in Canada," CBC News, April 21, 2009, http://www.cbc.ca/canada/ story/2009/04/01/f-biker-gangs. html (Accessed September 29, 2009); Gangsters Incorporated, "The Great Northern Biker War," http://gangstersinc.tripod.com/ Biker.html (Accessed November 8, 2008).

22. Ed Pilkington, "Former US Mafia boss John Gotti Jr. arrested in New York," *Guardian* (London), August 5, 2008; Virtual Ginza, "The Yakuza," http://www.virtual ginza.com/okinawa.htm?yakuza. htm (Accessed September 29, 2009); Peter Lilley, "Organized crime: The global business success story," Proximal Consulting, http://www.proximalconsulting .com/Pages/Organized%20 Crime%20INC/organize d%20 crime%20inc_pp (Accessed November 8, 2008).

23. National Criminal Justice Reference Center, http://www.ncjrs. gov/spotlight/gangs/facts.html (Accessed November 8, 2008).

Chapter 4

1. DEA press release, http://www. usdoj.gov/dea/pubs/pressrel/ pr091708.html (Posted September 17, 2008).

2. Ibid.

3. Martin Booth, *Opium: A History* (New York: St. Martin's, 1996), 191–197; Alfred McCoy, *The Politics of Heroin* (New York: Lawrence Hill, 1991), 88.

4. National Public Radio, "Timeline: America's War on Drugs," http://www.npr.org/templates/ story/story.php?storyId=9252490 (Accessed November 10, 2008).

5. Timeline: America's War on Drugs; Constitution of the United States, Article 1, Section 9.

6. Dan Moldea, *Dark Victory* (New York: Viking, 1986), 322, 326–327, 331.

7. McCoy, *Politics of Heroin*, 53–70.

8. Ibid., 122–124.

9. Jim Marrs, *Crossfire* (New York: Carroll & Graf, 1989), 135–210.

10. McCoy, 193–261.

11. Jonathan Kwitny, *The Crimes of Patriots* (New York: W.W. Norton, 1987); Peter Scott and Jonathan Marshall, *Cocaine Politics* (Berkeley: University of California Press, 1991).

12. Alexander Cockburn and Jeffrey St. Clair, *Whiteout: The CIA, Drugs and the Press* (New York: Verso, 1998), 1–62; Sam Stanton, "Reporter's suicide confirmed by coroner," *Sacramento Bee,* December 15, 2004.

13. Ali Mokdad, James Marks, Donna Stoup, and Julie Gerberding, "Actual causes of death in the United States, 2000," *Journal of the American Medical Association* 291 (March 10, 2004): 1242.

14. Bureau of Justice Statistics, http:// www.ojp.usdoj.gov/bjs/dcf/duc.

htm#drug-related (Accessed August 26, 2009).

15. Ibid.

16. "Briefing: How Mexico is waging war on drug cartels," *Christian Science Monitor,* August 16, 2009.

17. "Drug War Clock," Drug Sense, http://www.drugsense.org/wod clock.htm (Accessed November 10, 2008).

18. Buddy T., "Drug overdose deaths double in five years," About.com, http://alcoholism.about.com/od/prescription/a/overdose.htm (Accessed November 10, 2008).

19. Bureau of Justice Statistics, http://www.ojp.usdoj.gov/bjs/dcf/duc.htm#drug-related (Accessed November 10, 2008).

20. National Institute on Alcohol Abuse and Alcoholism, http://www.niaaa.nih.gov; DWI Statistics, http://www.nh-dwi.com/caip-206.htm (Accessed November 10, 2008).

21. Centers for Disease Control and Prevention, "Fire Deaths and Injuries: Fact Sheet," http://www.cdc.gov/ncipc/factsheets/fire.htm (Accessed November 10, 2008).

22. WrongDiagnosis.com, "Deaths from cirrhosis of the liver," http://www.wrongdiagnosis. com/c/cirrhosis_of_the_liver/deaths.htm (Accessed November 10, 2008); Centers for Disease Control, "Reported cirrhosis mortality—United States, 1970-1980, http://www.cdc.gov/mmwr/preview/mmwrhtml/00000440.htm (Accessed November 10, 2008); Alcohol Poisoning Statistics, http://www.whatisalcoholpoisoning.com/alcohol-poisoning-statistics.html (Accessed November 10, 2008).

23. Bureau of Justice Statistics, http://www.ojp.usdoj.gov/bjs/pub/pdf/ac.pdf (Accessed November 10, 2008).

24. U.S. Fire Administration, http://www.usfa.dhs.gov/campaigns/smoking (Accessed November 10, 2008); Bio-Medicine, http://www.bio-medicine.org/medicine-news/Annual-Tobacco-related-Deaths-to-Reach-8-3-Million-by-2030-23926-1 (Accessed November 10, 2008).

25. Mark Jacobson, "The return of Superfly," *New York Magazine,* http://nymag.com/ny metro/news/people/features/3649 (Posted August 7, 2000).

26. Ibid.

27. National Public Radio, "Timeline: America's War on Drugs," http://www.npr.org/templates/story/story.php? storyId=9252490 (Accessed November 10, 2008); Drug Policy Education Group, *Drug Policy News* 2, 1 (Spring/Summer 2001): 5.

Chapter 5

1. Texans for Public Justice, "Bush Donor Profile," http://www.tpj.org/docs/pioneers/pioneers_vi ew.jsp?id=38 (Accessed November 6, 2008).

2. "The Rise and Fall of Enron," *New York Times,* http://www.nytimes.com/ref/business/20060201_ENRON_GRAPHIC.html (Accessed November 6, 2008).

3. "Thalidomide," Medic8.com, http://www.medic8.com/medicines/Thalidomide.html (Accessed November 6, 2008).

4. David Armstrong, "How the New England Journal missed warning signs on Vioxx," *Wall Street Journal*, May 15, 2006.

5. Armstrong, *Wall Street Journal*, May 15, 2006.

6. "China executes the former head of its food and drug agency," *International Herald Tribune*, July 10, 2007; "Chinese toy boss 'kills himself'," BBC News, http://news.bbc.co.uk/2/hi/6943689.stm (Posted August 13, 2007).

7. "Rise and Fall of Enron."

8. Federal Bureau of Investigation, "Fourth quarter bank robbery statistics show slight uptick," http://www.fbi.gov/pressrel/pressrel08/bankstats072808.htm (Posted July 28, 2008).

9. Sandy Shore, "Adelphia Communications to sell long-distance phone service," *Pittsburgh Post-Gazette,* July 6, 2005.

10. "Adelphia founder John Rigas found guilty," MSNBC, http://www.msnbc.msn.com/id/5396406 (Accessed August 26, 2009).

11. Stephen Taub, "Probation for Adelphia's Michael Rigas," CFO.com, http://www.cfo.com/article.cfm/5598021/c_5591729?f=TodayInFinance_Inside (Accessed August 26, 2009).

12. Shore, "Adelphia sells long-distance service for $1.2 million," *Denver Business Journal,* July 6, 2005.

13. Nathan Miller, *Stealing from America* (New York: Paragon, 1992), 347.

14. Nathaniel Nash, "Showdown time for Danny Wall," *New York Times,* July 9, 1989.

15. Timothy Curry and Lynn Shibut, "The Cost of the Savings and Loan Crisis," FDIC.gov, http://www.fdic.gov/bank/analytical/banking/2000dec/brv13n2_2.pdf (Accessed November 6, 2008).

16. U.S. Senate, "Preliminary inquiry into allegations regarding Senators Cranston, DeConcini, Glenn, McCain, and Riegle, and Lincoln Savings and Loan: Open session hearings before the Select Committee on Ethics," November 15, 1990, through January 16, 1991.

17. Louise Dubose, "O, Brother! Where Art Thou!" *Austin Chronicle,* March 16, 2001.

18. Colin Barr, "Bank bailout could cost $4 trillion," *Forbes*, http://money.cnn.com/20 09/01/27/news/bigger.bailout.fortune (Posted January 27, 2009).

19. David Johnston, "Investigator finds evidence of crimes in House Bank use," *New York Times,* December 17, 1992.

20. "General Electric," CorpWatch, http://www.corpwatch.org/section.php?id=16 (Accessed November 6, 2008); Mark Zepezauer and Arthur Naiman, *Take the Rich Off Welfare* (Tucson: Odonian Press, 1996), 19–20.

21. Project on Government Oversight, "The Politics of Contracting," POGO, http://www.pogo.org/p/contracts/c/co-030608-ge.html (Accessed November 6, 2008).

22. Jeff Gerth and Brady Dennis, "How a loophole benefits GE in bank rescue," *Washington Post*, June 29, 2009.

23. Zepezauer and Naiman, 18–19.

24. William Blum, *Killing Hope* (Monroe, Maine: Common Courage Press, 1995), 72–83.

25. David Lynch, "Murder and payoffs taint business in Colombia," *USA Today,* October 30, 2007.

26. "ImClone stock sales disclosed," *New York Times,* July 15, 2002.

27. "Chiquita sued in NY over killings in Colombia," Reuters, http://www.reuters. com/article/americasCrisis/idUSN14211578 (Accessed August 28, 2009).

28. CCAJAR—Editorial, "Extradition cut short," Colectivo de Abogados, http://www.colectivodeabogados. org/EXTRA DITION-CUT-SHORT (Accessed August 26, 2009).

Chapter 6

1. Guy Lawson and William Oldham, *The Brotherhoods: The True Story of Two Cops Who Murdered for the Mafia* (New York: Scribner, 2006).

2. Anthony Lukas, *Nightmare: The Underside of the Nixon Years* (New York: Viking, 1976); Anthony Summers, *The Arrogance of Power* (New York: Penguin, 2001).

3. PBS Frontline, "The Rampart Scandal," PBS, http://www.pbs. org/wgbh/pages /frontline/shows/lapd/scandal (Accessed November 8, 2008).

4. "The Exonerated," *Reader's Digest,* http://www.rd.com/your-america-inspiring-people-and-stories/the-exonerated-wrongful-conviction/article54253.html (Accessed November 8, 2008).

5. Richard Stengel, "Cover stories: Khashoggi's high-flying realm," *Time,* http://www.time. com/time/magazine/article/0,9171,963261,00.html (January 19, 1987).

6. Kevin Martin, "Real rogues: The big four corporate criminals," *Press for Conversion!* (December 2004): 36; "Lockheed drops Titan merger after delays by bribery probe," *Los Angeles Times,* June 27, 2004.

7. Curt Gentry, *J. Edgar Hoover: The Man and the Secrets* (New York: Plume, 1992), 109–123.

8. Transparency International, *Global Corruption Report 2004* (London: Pluto Press, 2004), 1443–1476.

9. Hecor Feliciano, *The Lost Museum* (New York: Harper Collins, 1997); Lynn Nicholas, *The Rape of Europa* (London: Macmillan, 1994).

Chapter 7

1. Institute for War and Peace Reporting, "Bosnia's 'Book of the Dead,'" iwpr.net, http://www.iwpr.net/?p=tri&s=f&o=3365 66&apc_state=henh (Accessed November 8, 2008).

2. "Bosnia: Mass graves with Serb victims found," *Tanjug,* August 5, 2008.

3. London Charter of the International Military Tribunal (August 8, 1945), paragraphs 6a-6c.

4. Rome Statute of the International Criminal Court, Article 7.

5. George Rosie, *The Directory of International Terrorism* (Edinburgh: Mainstream, 1986), 22.

6. Robert Conquest, *The Great Terror* (New York: Macmillan, 1969).

7. Philip Short, *Mao: A Life* (New York: Macmillan, 2000), 761.

8. David Gwyn, *Idi Amin: Death-Light of Africa* (Boston: Little, Brown, 1977).

9. Heraldo Munoz, *The Dictator's Shadow* (New York: Basic Books, 2008).

10. Raphael Lemkin, *Axis Rule in Occupied Europe* (Washington, D.C.: Carnegie Endowment for International Peace, 1944).

11. United Nations Convention on the Prevention and Punishment of the Crime of Genocide (1948), Article 2.

12. "Germany admits Namibia genocide," BBC News, http://news.bbc.co.uk/2/hi/africa/3565938.stm (Accessed August 28, 2009); "Swiss accept Armenia 'genocide,'" BBC News, http://news.bbc.co.uk/2/hi/europe/3325247.stm (Accessed August 28, 2009); Foreign Office Memorandum by Mr. G.W. Rendel on Turkish Massacres and Persecutions of Minorities since the Armistice, March 20, 1922; Robert Gellately, *Lenin, Stalin, and Hitler* (New York: Knopf, 2007), 70–71; Helen Fawkes, "Legacy of famine divides Ukraine," BBC News, http://news.bbc.co.uk/2/hi/europe/6179818.stm (Accessed August 28, 2009).

13. Martin Gilbert, *Atlas of the Holocaust* (New York: William Morrow, 1993); InfoPlease.com, "Casualties in World War II," http://www.infoplease.com/ipa/A0004619.html (Accessed November 8, 2008).

14. "Guatemala 'genocide' probe blames state," BBC News, http://news.bbc.co.uk/2/hi/americas/286402.stm (Accessed August 28, 2009); Anthony Mascarenhas, Bangladesh: A Legacy of Blood (London: Hodder and Stoughton, 1986); Sian Powell, "UN verdict on East Timor," *The Australian*, January 19, 2006; Les Neuhaus, "Ethiopian dictator sentenced to prison," FoxNews.com, http://www.foxnews.com/printer_friendly_wires/2007Jan11/0,4675,EthiopiaDictatoraprossTrial,00.html, (Posted January 11, 2007).; "Rwanda: How the genocide happened," BBC News, http://news.bbc.co.uk/2/hi/africa/1288230.stm (Accessed August 28, 2009).

15. Allan Hall, "Eichmann memoirs published," *The Guardian* (London), August 12, 1999.

16. International Criminal Court, Rome Statute (2002), Part I, Article 8.

17. Cambodian Genocide Group, http://www.cambodiangenocide.org/genocide.htm (Accessed November 8, 2008).

18. Review and recommendation of the deputy judge advocate for war crimes, October 20, 1947; "Murder in the name of war—My Lai," BBC News, http://news.bbc.co.uk/2/hi/special_report/1998/03/98/mylai/64344.stm (Accessed August 28, 2009).

Chapter 8

1. FBI Press Release, http://www.fbi.gov/pressrel/pressrel08/bankstats072808.htm (Posted July 28, 2008).

2. Internet Crime Complaint Center, 2007 Internet Crime Report, http://www.ic3.gov/media/annualreport/2007_IC3Report.pdf (Accessed November 10, 2008).

3. Scamdex, "Advance Fee Fraud," Scamdex, The Email Scam Resource, http://www.scamdex.

com/419-index.php (Accessed November 10, 2008).

4. Jacquelin Magnay, "Ticket swindle leaves trail of losers," *Sydney Morning Herald*, August 4, 2008.

5. Bob Sullivan, "Survey: 2 million bank accounts robbed," MSNBC, http://www.msnbc.msn.com/id/5184077/ (Posted June 14, 2004).

6. Andrew Kramer, "Online Nordic banking theft stirs talk of Russian hacker," *New York Times*, January 25, 2007.

7. Fiona Raisbeck, "Gang arrested on suspicion of $300,000 Internet bank theft," *SC Magazine*, http://www.scmagazineuk.com/Gang-arrested-on-suspicion-of-300000-internet-bank-theft/article/106137 (Accessed November 10, 2008).

8. Jerry Ropelato, "Internet Pornography Statistics," TopTenReviews.com, http://www.internet-filter-review.toptenreviews.com/internet-pornography-statistics.html (Accessed November 10, 2008).

9. "Child porn gang face jail," CNN, http://archives.cnn.com/2001/WORLD/europ e/UK/02/13/england.pornography/index.html (Accessed August 28, 2009).

10. "Tracking child porn," BBC News, http://news.bbc.co.uk/2/hi/uk_news/2445065.stm (Accessed August 28, 2009).

11. Ibid.

12. Cormac O'Keeffe, "Nationwide swoop followed FBI tip-off," *Irish Examiner*, April 24, 2004.

13. "Operation Auxin explained," *Sydney Morning Herald*, September 30, 2004.

14. FBI, "Innocent Images National Initiative," http://www.fbi.gov/publications/innocent.htm (Accessed November 10, 2008).

15. U.S. Immigration and Customs Enforcement, "Operation Predator," http://www.ice.gov/pi/predator/newsreleases.htm (Accessed November 10, 2008).

16. Virtual Global Taskforce, http://www.virtualglobaltaskforce.com/latest_news.asp (Accessed November 10, 2008).

17. Boyd Clark, "Profile: Gary McKinnon," BBC News, http://news.bbc.co.uk/2/hi /uk_news/7839338.stm (Accessed August 28, 2009).

18. Ibid.

19. "Cyber-terrorism will be punishable by death," *Daily Times* (Lahore, Pakistan), November 7, 2008.

20. Sophos.com, "Melissa virus writer pleads guilty," http://www.sophos.com/pressoffice/ news/articles/1999/12/va_melissa.html (Accessed November 10, 2008).

21. "Mafiaboy given eight months," *The Register (London),* September 13, 2001.

Chapter 9

1. Death Penalty Information Center, "Some examples of post-Furman botched executions," http://www.deathpenaltyinfo.org/some-examples-post-furman-botched-executions (Accessed November 10, 2008).

2. Ibid.

3. Bureau of Justice Statistics, http://www.ojp.usdoj.gov/bjs/prisons.htm (Accessed November 10, 2008); U.S. Census Bureau, http://factfinder.census.gov (Accessed November 10, 2008).

4. Adam Liptak, "U.S. prison population dwarfs that of other nations,"

International Herald Tribune,
April 23, 2008.

5. FBI Uniform Crime Reports,
http://www.fbi.gov/ucr/ucr.htm
(Accessed November 10, 2008).

6. Bureau of Justice Statistics, http://
www.ojp.usdoj.gov/bjs/crimoff.
htm#recidivism (Accessed
November 10, 2008).

7. "Executions in the U.S. 1608–
2002: The Espy File," Death
Penalty Information Center,
http://www.deathpenaltyinfo.org/
executions-us-1608-2002-espy-file
(Accessed November 10, 2008);
Death Penalty Information Center, http://deathpenaltyinfo.org/
executions (Accessed November
10, 2008).

8. "History of the Death Penalty,"
Death Penalty Information Center, http://www.deathpenaltyinfo.
org/part-i-history-death-penalty
(Accessed November 10, 2008).

9. The Innocence Project, http://
www.innocenceproject.org/
Content/351.php (Accessed
November 10, 2008); Jeff Flock,
"Blanket commutation empties
Illinois death row," CNN, January
13, 2003, http://www.stopcapital
punishment.org/coverage/46.html
(Accessed September 29, 2009)

10. *Furman v. Georgia,* 408 U.S. 238
(1972).

11. Joan Cheever, *Back from the Dead*
(New York: John Wiley & Sons,
2006).

12. Death Penalty Information Center, "Facts about the Death Penalty," http://www.deathpenalty
info.org/documents/FactSheet.
pdf (Accessed September 29,
2009).

13. Jennifer McMenamin, "Death
penalty costs Md. more than life
term," *Baltimore Herald*, March 6,
2008; "Costs of the Death Penalty,"
Death Penalty Information Center,
http://www.deathpenaltyinfo.org/
costs-death-penalty (Accessed
November 10, 2008).

14. Chris Suellentrop, "How Often
Do Prisoners Escape?" Slate,
http://www.slate.com/id/1007001/
(Accessed November 10, 2008);
"Fact Sheet: Corrections Safety,"
Association of State Correctional
Administrators, http://www.asca.
net/documents/FACTSHEET.
pdf (Accessed November 10,
2008); Florida Department of
Corrections, http://www.dc.state.
fl.us/pub/annual/0506/stats/im_
escapes.html (Accessed November
10, 2008).

Bibliography

Fichtelberg, Aaron. *Crime Without Borders: An Introduction to International Criminal Justice*. Upper Saddle River, N.J.: Prentice Hall, 2007.

Friedman, Lawrence. *Crime And Punishment In American History*. Jackson, Tenn: Basic Books, 1994.

Friedrichs, David. *Trusted Criminals: White Collar Crime in Contemporary Society*. Florence, Ky.: Wadsworth, 2006.

Lunde, Paul. *Organized Crime: An Inside Guide to the World's Most Successful Industry*. New York: DK Books, 2004.

Miller, Nathan. *Stealing from America: A History of Corruption from Jamestown to Reagan*. New York: Paragon House, 1992.

Oliver, Willard, and James Hilgenberg Jr. *A History of Crime and Criminal Justice in America*. Upper Saddle River, N.J.: Prentice Hall, 2005.

Roth, Mitchel. *Crime and Punishment: A History of the Criminal Justice System*. Florence, Ky.: Wadsworth, 2004.

Wilson, Colin. *A Criminal History of Mankind*. London, Mercury, 2005.

Further Resources

Clear, Todd, George Cole, and Michael Reisig. *American Corrections.* Florence, Ky.: Wadsworth, 2008.

Morash, Merry. *Understanding Gender, Crime, and Justice.* Thousand Oaks, Calif.: Sage, 2005.

Weisburd, David, and Chester Britt. *Statistics in Criminal Justice.* New York: Springer, 2007.

Internet

Crime Library
http://www.trutv.com/library/crime/index.html

Federal Bureau of Investigation
http://www.fbi.gov/

USA History: Crime
http://www.spartacus.schoolnet.co.uk/USAcrime.htm

Index

About the Author

Michael Newton has published 215 books since 1977, with 21 forthcoming from various houses through 2011. His history of the Florida Ku Klux Klan (*The Invisible Empire,* 2001) won the Florida Historical Society's 2002 Rembert Patrick Award for "Best Book in Florida History," and his *Encyclopedia of Cryptozoology* was one of the American Library Association's Outstanding Reference Works in 2006. His nonfiction work includes *The Encyclopedia of American Law Enforcement, The Encyclopedia of Serial Killers, The Encyclopedia of Unsolved Crimes,* and many other books for Facts on File.